RADICAL VEGETARIANISM

RADICAL VEGETARIANISM

A Dialectic of Diet and Ethic

Mark Mathew Braunstein

Lantern Books • New York
A Division of Booklight, Inc.

2010

Lantern Books

128 Second Place

Brooklyn, NY 11231

www.lanternbooks.com

Copyright © 1981, 1993, 2010 by Mark M. Braunstein.

All rights reserved. No part of this book may be reproduced, stored
in a retrieval system, or transmitted in any form or by any means,
electronic, mechanical, photocopying, recording, or otherwise,
without the written permission of Lantern Books.

Frontispiece by Hans Sebald Beham, "Adam and Eve," 1535;
Page 23, illustration by Pieter Brueghel the Elder, "Big Fish Eat Little Fish," 1556;
Page 144 illustration by Pieter Brueghel the Elder,
"The Rich Kitchen" & "The Impoverished Kitchen," 1563;
Page 187, illustration by Jean Jacques Grandville, from his book
Scenes from the Private & Public Lives of the Animals, 1842.

LIBRARY OF CONGRESS CATALOGING-IN-PUBLICATION DATA

Braunstein, Mark Mathew, 1951–
 Radical vegetarianism : a dialectic of diet and ethic / Mark
Mathew Braunstein.—Rev. ed.
  p. cm.
 Includes bibliographical references.
 ISBN-13: 978-1-59056-151-5 (alk. paper)
 ISBN-10: 1-59056-151-1 (alk. paper)
 1. Vegetarianism. I. Title.
TX392.B72 2009
641.5'636—dc22

2009024467

Contents

To

Elsie the Cow
Porky Pig
Mary's little lamb
Chicken Little
Donald Duck
Charlie the Tuna

and also much Cattle
(Jonah 4:6)

Preface

DESPITE OUR TWO EYES, we see in only one direction. Where we do not look, we do not see. Our intellect, too, ponders only where we direct it. Now a vegetarian, you previously may have been a carnivore. Before converting, you possibly never suspected your future. If some evangelist nutritionist or animal rights activist espoused a reason for closing your mouth to flesh foods, who believed it? Now that you do believe it, your conviction does not entitle you to close your eyes.

Are your shoes made of leather? During famine, carnivores have resorted to cooking and eating their shoes. Cowhide is presently a by-product of hamburger. But if cows were killed just for their skins, their flesh would be no more morally edible just because you did not wear leather.

Do you perceive the veal floating invisibly inside every glass of milk? A dairy cow is not killed outright, but condemning her to cruel conditions might be worse than saving her skin. Meanwhile her calf, briefly confined, is killed. The dairy barn adjoins the veal crate. Dairy Queen is merged in discorporate partnership with Burger King. Every cup of milk is appetizer to a meal of veal. If your lips are white with milk, your hands are red with blood.

Do you feel the chicken heart beating silently in every egg? The heart is the hen's, not her chick's. A hen never once sees the sun, never once has any husband to peck, and forever counts her chickens before they hatch.

Why buy corn from Colonel Sanders or potatoes from Wendy or fries from Ronald McDonald if you would not buy wieners from Oscar Meyer or wings from Frank Perdue? Dining on the salad bar in a charcoal charnel steakhouse, you eat lettuce and tomatoes yet smell flesh and bones. Where everyone else busily buries in their stomachs the dead bodies on their plates, that is not a meal, it is a funeral. You try to be sociable but, out of respect for the dead, you keep your silence.

Keep your peas, but why your peace? From canned food and TV dinners in microwaves to canned laughter on TV airwaves, and from politicians' platitudes to physicians' placebos, our sick society denies nature's truths, a blind donkey ignoring an organic carrot.

Proving the superfluity of protein from eggs or minerals from milk or fats from fish, we vegans thrive our long lives upon plain plants. This is the vegetarian dialectic of diet and ethic: not coincidentally, but absolutely essentially, those foods that deprive the fewest lives from others contribute to the longest lives for ourselves.

Thus this polemic aims to persuade ethical vegetarians of the moral necessity of health, and to convince those concerned about nutrition to consider also the unhealthy consequences of perdition.

Between the many questions of philosophies and the few answers of recipes, between the religious and the delicious, we slice our fruits and vegetables along the sharp edge between life and death. Indeed these are vegetarianism's subjects: not just fruits and vegetables, but life and death.

M.M.B.

Mamacoke Island, CT

PART ONE: DIET

You can believe me or not as you like; but truths are not such tough old Methuselahs as most people imagine. A normal, ordinary truth is good for, say, seventeen or eighteen—at most twenty years; seldom more. And truths as venerable as that are nothing but skin and bones; yet it isn't until then that the great majority adopts them and prescribes them to Society as wholesome spiritual food. But there's not much nourishment in that kind of diet, I assure you; as a doctor you can take my word for that. These tired old truths are as rancid and moldy as last year's bacon; they're the cause of all that moral scurvy that plagues Society.

HENRIK IBSEN
An Enemy of the People

I.

NUTRITION IN THE LIGHT
OF VEGETARIANISM

*The popular medical formulation of morality that goes
back to Ariston of Chios, "virtue is the health of the soul,"
would have to be changed to become useful, at least to
read: "your virtue is the health of your soul." For there is
no health as such, and all attempts to define a thing that
way have been wretched failures. Even the determination
of what is healthy for your body depends on your goal,
your horizon, your energies, your impulses, your errors,
and above all on the ideals and the phantasms of your
soul. Thus there are innumerable healths of the body; and
the more we allow the unique and incomparable to raise
its head again, and the more we abjure the dogma of the
"equality of men," the more must the concept of a normal
health, along with a normal diet and the normal course
of an illness, be abandoned by medical men. Only then
would the time have come to reflect on the health and
illness of the soul, and to find the peculiar virtue of each
man in the health of his soul. In one person, of course,
this health could look like its opposite in another person.*

Friedrich Nietzsche
The Gay Science,
Book III Number 120

A MERICANS LOVE ANIMALS: as pets, in zoos, at circuses, in the wild, and on farms. Americans especially love farm animals: for breakfast, lunch, and dinner.

As mostly urbanites, for many of us our only contact with animals that we so much profess to love is at the tip of a fork or at the bottom of a spoon. We commonly query about our food: Is it organic? or, What is its sodium content? or, How much added salt? or, How many extra calories? But some questions we neglect to ask, questions such as: How much blood, sweat, or tears were shed for this food? and, Whose blood? and, Whose sweat? and, Whose tears? Our answers can be only as good as our questions.

"What must we eat so that we are not merely the product of what we eat?" asks Rudolf Steiner in a lecture entitled *Nutritional Questions in the Light of Spiritual Science*, translated tersely as *Problems of Nutrition*, but that simply could have been called *Problems*. *What Does It Mean to Be a Vegetarian?* could be the title of our book at hand, and *What Does It Mean to Be Healthy?* and *What Does It Mean to Be Moral?* could be its two halves' subtitles. In the end, we are really concerned about "Moral Health" or "Health of the Soul." But this is only the beginning.

Every ethnic group possesses its own foods, and often its own diseases. Thus for supervision in these matters we can no longer look to our parents. Nor can we look to our friends who, in one breath apologize for the flesh on their plates, yet in the next breath swallow it. Sometimes they eat faster in the presence of vegetarians, as though wishing to end the subject as quickly as possible. Nor can we look to animals. Though we look like apes, we do not live like apes, so we cannot eat like apes. Even two apes eat differently from each other if one lives in an African jungle, while the other dwells in an American zoo. If we were to imitate either's diet, it would have to be that of the latter, the prisoner behind bars. Some might consider any emphasis on food completely irrelevant: the person who eats beer and franks with cheer and thanks just might live longer than someone who eats pears and sprouts with fears and doubts.

Health, however, is not merely long life, but also complete freedom from disease, no matter how long or short the life. One who lives for fifty years in good health with the least possible sleep has already lived longer than one in ill health for seventy-five years, much of it in pain and most of it in bed. Swift describes in *Gulliver's Travels* the immortal Struldbruggs of the land of the Luggnaggians who were doomed to eternal senility since they could not die. Apollo granted the Sibyl of Cumae life for as many grains of sand as she held in her hand. But she was not so wise in her youth as when Aeneas met her seven hundred years later, for she had neglected to ask for beauty and health along with immortality. "I want to die," she told those who visited her. Parodied in jingle and rhyme: "Spirulina / and sprouted wheat bread / Will make you live so long / You'll wish you were dead."

The best possible nutrition alone cannot ensure the best possible health, nor does the worst sort of food distinctively cause the worst health. Nevertheless, the major cause of illness is poor nutrition. Samuel Butler describes in *Erewhon* a utopian society where the sick are put in jails, not hospitals, since sickness is a crime as much against humanity as against the hindered individual. Disease is not some crime for which one is punished, but is itself the punishment for another crime. Poor nutrition is the crime; poor health is consequently the punishment.

Civilization's last hope of survival rests on every individual's first hope: proper nutrition. In Germany today, as in *Erewhon*, the sick are sent to the reform house, *reformhaus* meaning in German the "health food store." In England and Switzerland and Canada today, addicts of heroin—white and refined much like flour and sugar—are hospitalized. Yet hospitalization is not without risks, for an examination of patients' meals shows that many dieticians are as ill informed as most patients. There, too, is the domain of doctors of medicine, which is to say doctors of disease, since medicine is a science concerned only with regaining, not maintaining, health.

Donors are advised by doctors neither to smoke tobacco nor to drink alcohol for one hour after giving blood, and before departure from the lab are given coffee and donuts. Were the doctors as much concerned with body types as with blood types, they would advise never to smoke or drink and would instead provide a piece of fruit. Who is still fool enough to take seriously modern medicine's advice in matters of health, and therefore of life and death? Those defrauded by Western nutrition the first half of their lives are destined to be victimized by Western medicine the second half.

State sales taxes are often levied upon all but the very essential. Thus in some states food and drugs are defined as such absolute necessities, while in others only the drugs go untaxed. Official dogma would have us believe it is more important to cure a disease than to prevent it, and that drugs are more sustaining than food.

No medicine has ever cured the body of a disease, but then neither has any food; rather, the body cures itself. All that a medicine or food can do is help the body to help itself. Better to depend on food, the twice- or thrice-daily answer to the constant question the body poses. Magnesium, calcium, and the rest of the nutrients essential to life, if isolated as pills in a chemically pure form, cannot alone sustain life in any animal. They must be fed as found in food. Food in a highly refined form, devoid of elements naturally inherent in it, also barely sustains life. Life depends not on mere chart values found in books, but rather on intrinsic organic energy that unites a living cell with its elements, making it more than the sum of its parts. This *more* is the life force, called *chi* in the East, and *vibes* in the West.

Nutritionists make claims about pills' nutritional equivalency with food, but never speak about spiritual equivalency. This spirit is impossible to define; it is, by nature, ineffable. It plumbs depths that the mind's eye barely sees and that the intellect senses only obliquely, yet its effects are as apparent as the healthy glow on a face. Experienced health food salespeople know by that look whether a customer has come to purchase real food or vitamin pills.

We must learn to eat with judgment, to digest with deliberation, at all times to eat the right food, and at the right times to eat no food. Ultimately and endlessly, eating requires as much care and intelligence as reading. Instead of reading *War and Peace,* some save time and read a synopsis. Likewise, instead of eating real food, some follow the American tradition of popping pills. Vitamin pills are supplements, not substitutes. Similarly, no one who reads a synopsis can hope to experience the revelations and frustrations of Pierre, Natasha, and Prince Andrei.

All through life we read books and eat food. Early in life we should read books about eating food. We need invest only half a year searching for a suitable system of nutrition to be repaid a dividend of half a lifetime at maturation. But study as we may, we must remember that what one nutritionist writes is right for one person only: that nutritionist. No reader should follow a diet because an author follows it (if, indeed, the author follows it). Rather, students should read a hundred books and formulate one plan from them, just as each author had done in reading a thousand books, devising ten diets, and writing one book. In the end, though, every diet is false. No matter what we eat, we die. Thus, that system that promotes the longest life is merely the least at fault.

Where neophyte vegetarians go wrong nutritionally is not in having omitted flesh, but in continuing to eat everything else as before without care of substitution for the omission. Their ill health stands as an example for carnivores to point to in rationalizing their diets. (The common practice of exhibiting the unhealthiest specimens of the different regimens as standards is equivalent to establishing rules through their exceptions.) Consider the classic plastic fast food meal of burgers, fries, Coke, and pies. Never mind that the potatoes are fried in left-over hamburger fat, that the Coke contains sugar whose refining uses animal bone, that the pie crust is often made with animal shortening, called simply lard. Eliminate the burger and the diner is deprived of the one vestige of nutrition in the meal; if the meal minus the meat is still eaten, its constant repetition can only cause degeneration into sickness. Though healthy vegetarians are generally healthier than healthy carnivores, unhealthy vegetarians generally are unhealthier. The one step of leaving out flesh is not a deed that makes any future act superfluous. The average vegetarian must possess a little more than average knowledge about nutrition.

If we have abandoned eating flesh so that others might find more on the bones they pick, we must still investigate nutrition and, in the process, abandon eating garbage: white flour, white sugar, white shortening, white baking powder, white salt, white milk (piece of cake!) and so on down the line of what should be whitewashed down the drain. As important as knowing what to eat is knowing what not to eat. Until recently in grade school, children were taught the four basic food groups: meat, poultry, and fish; eggs, milk, and dairy products; fruits and vegetables; and nuts, seeds, and grains. Teachers said we needed a daily selection from each group, and being children their schoolchildren believed them. But those grown too old to be their students now realize that they were too foolish to have been their teachers. What they called nutrition, we now call gluttony.

Where there is no choice, there is no sacrifice. Some would as readily eat monkey meat if it were made available in their markets, or cat flesh if it became common, as they do lamb legs (under an inverted guise called *leg of lamb*) and cutup calves (under a guise called *veal cutlet*). That the apes occupy rungs so near to ours on the evolutionary ladder is not the only reason they do not find their way into culinary ladles; rather, with so many ending on laboratory tables, hardly enough are left for butcher blocks. And because dogs and cats play next door is not the only reason they do not end in the next meal; rather, they, too, eat flesh, so their own does not taste as good as the vegetarian farm and fish animals they are given to eat. Modern day humans eat not so much out of choice as out of convenience.

American carnivorism fits right in with American consumerism, and it is the American way of eating with which we are specifically concerned. Differences exist in carnivorism between one geographic or economic area and another. For instance, Asia differs so greatly from America that the question should be considered whether the same term should even apply to both. The point is that an Asian carnivore shares more in common with an American vegetarian than with an American carnivore. Most Europeans eat flesh frequently but not heavily, sprinkling specks here and there into their grains and into their vegetables; but Americans, Australians and Argentines—the people of the three great cattle countries— eat grains and vegetables mostly as side dishes.

The typical American carnivore consumes flesh at least once a day and as much as once a meal; whereas the average Asian indulges no more than once a week, maybe once a month, and in fish flesh and sea meats at that. Few national cuisines emphasize the ingredient of flesh so obsessively as ours. Thus, the carnivorism referred to henceforth shall be the affluent American type, both because of its extreme example and its particular relevance.

Carnivores can be healthy, and health itself is important, but more important is its attainment at the least effort and expense. For true health is maintained not by the development of will power but by the elimination of inessentials. If good health can be achieved from elimination of one food group, namely pieces of dead animals (meat, poultry, fish and sea meats), then maybe better health could come from eliminating another group, namely products of live animals (eggs, milk and dairy).

"Baloney!" the reader might gasp, but the Five Books of Moses admonish us not to cook a kid in its mother's milk, a kind of respect for the dead but not yet buried. Kosher and other Semitic dietary laws prohibiting the mixing of meat and milk imply the inadvisability of each alone, like alcohol and barbiturates (but not like fruits and vegetables, which one should eat, but not together). Perhaps the analogy totters on the tenuous. While a book read is not a life led, we should keep in mind that those nutritionists—whether self-decreed or college-degreed—whose views demand what appears difficult are precisely the ones worth reading. That something is difficult might be more reason to try to do it. After all, vegetarianism is difficult, but only within the confines of a carnivorous society, and then only at first, like fasting: the fast the first day, vegetarianism the first year. Nutrition and health writers who do not condemn cadaver consumption may be hesitant to ask what is difficult of their readership, since they are writing commercially for large audiences.

Most diet authors say next to nothing about carnivorism, and nothing about vegetarianism. And some say less than nothing. Oriented toward the easy, they are well rewarded for their orthodox views. In his book *A Diet for Living* (page 184), Jean Mayer, while seated sweetly on his Harvard chair endowed by the sugar industry, suggested that strict vegetarianism may stem from a "deep-seated psychological difficulty" and advised parents of children who will not eat meat to seek the services not of the school nutritionist, but of the school psychiatrist.

Carlton Fredericks, in his book *The Nutrition Handbook* (page 142), labels vegetarianism a "cult" that "represents more of a neurosis than a credo," and then asks: "Why avoid meat when a cow is merely walking grass?" Dear Mr. Fredericks: for that matter, "All flesh is grass" (Isaiah 40:6). Maybe a cow *is* walking grass. Let it walk. Let it walk of its own accord to its grave in the grass.

A cow would be nothing more than walking grass were it not for the cow spirit about her, just as Mr. Fredericks would be nothing more than a writing cow were it not for the human spirit about him. But ours is a materialistic society that places no value in spiritual matters because these cannot be boiled, bottled, and bought. That is the spirit's great fortune. This is a total fantasy, because no one type of food exists that the human body needs to eat; but just imagine for a moment that *not* eating something was unhealthful. Even *if* vegetarianism were proven unhealthful, many vegetarian parents concerned with matters beyond health would nevertheless refuse to feed to their children cows and calves, because calves, too, are cow's children.

Ours is a free as well as a materialistic society where advocates of the spirit can crusade against materialism as can vegetarians speak against carnivorism. Without even venturing into the 21st century, we can find eloquent spokespersons for vegetarianism among Klaper, Moran, Barnard, Shelton, Kulvinskas, Clement, Cousens, Diamond, McDougall, Wigmore, Ohsawa, Ehret, and Ornish. Paul Bragg, too, can be considered a vegetarian; he ate flesh whenever he wished...about once every ten years. Each of these book authors presents a system of vegetarian nutrition, none necessarily better than the other, and each unique. Though confusion might arise out of the diversity, many systems work, indeed any system works, a testament to both the wonders of the human body and the whole of nature.

All the above agree upon abstinence from flesh, and most upon abstinence from pills. Indeed, even the father of Western medicine, Hippocrates, advised us to leave drugs in the chemist's pot if we can be healed by food, so we first must know what the right food is. We need not know any system; knowing what is food is enough. For instance, George Ohsawa's macrobiotics prescribes mostly cooked grains and beans and proscribes most fruits; Herbert Shelton's natural hygiene prescribes mostly raw vegetables and raw fruits and proscribes all cooked grains and beans. Although opposite theories, each works for different people. The only one who should sternly follow Ohsawa's system is Ohsawa, or Shelton's system is Shelton; for their readers, eclecticism, not epigonism, should serve as their rule.

One reader might combine the two systems; that is, he eats mostly raw fruits and raw nuts and some raw vegetables during the summer, and mostly cooked grains and cooked beans with some cooked vegetables during the winter. Spring and fall are periods of transition as much for him as for the plants he eats. He aspires to a diet solely of fruits and nuts and sea vegetables: that which grows on the tops of trees and on the bottoms of seas, both the highest and lowest forms of vegetable life. All he or anyone might expect of vegetarianism in purely personal terms is that it promote a long, healthful life.

The description of real life as healthy life may be inadequate, but that of "health foods" as real foods is not. Some view "real foods" enthusiasts as selfish fetishists, not just concerned with their health but concerned *only* with their health. It is, however, no less selfish and far more wasteful to seek a cure for sickness caused by long years of eating fake foods. Furthermore, some complain that "real foods" do not taste good. But how could they know, when their bodies and sense organs have been desensitized by the consumption of meat and spicy and salty foods (and, perhaps, alcohol and tobacco as well)? Any food tastes better than aspirin and penicillin, which taste so terrible that rather than be chewed they must bypass the taste buds and be swallowed whole. Americans consume more meat and medication than any other nation, as though the practice of eating flesh preceded popping pills. The food in our lives is beneficial only as long as there is life in our food. A vitamin pill, synthetic or allegedly natural, may be comparable to that vitamin found in real food, but it is only one element and does little good if not combined with other nutrients.

Another misconception concerning real food is that, tasty or not, it hardly satisfies the appetite, an apparent cause of slimness among its adherents. Actually a slice of white bread supplies so few nutrients that the nutritionally starved diner is compelled to consume four or five slices where one slice of whole grain could suffice. Hence obesity is itself a sickness, a sort of "sufficiency disease."

There are many types of healthy people, many roots of and routes to health, many types of ill people, but few roots of and routes to illness: besides environmental and communicable and hereditary disease, much illness is deficiency disease. Regarding hereditary disease, even those illnesses may be linked to lack of proper food, since we tend to eat the same as our parents did. Modern medicine reflects modern materialism since it attributes diseases of the body to the presence of something from without, not the absence of something within.

We might worry that even real food does not supply sufficient nutrients, because the modern use of chemical fertilizers and food stabilizers may prolong shelf life, but not human life. But we need worry more for other reasons: what suffers most from the artificiality of modern technology is not our food but our lives. We must truly earn our food not with mere money but with sweat, for to eat enough to ensure salubrity without obesity, we must engage in adequate exercise. This could mean an early morning jog. One reason Americans most often exercise early in the morning is that it is the only time their stomachs are empty. To be able to exercise enough we must eat only those foods that do not weigh us down, thus eschewing fatty flesh food. If we are unable to dash away from the table after a meal, maybe we should not have sat down in the first place. The average vegetarian is two to ten kilograms slimmer than the average carnivore, and the average carnivore is just as much overweight; such a statistic affirms not the health of vegetarians, but the ill health of carnivores. If we as vegetarians eat less, we still are eating as much as we want of all we want; a healthy human neither needs nor wants too much food.

Good nutrition is only a few rungs up the ladder from bad nutrition. The ladder has no end, at least not within sight, as we stumble up each rung: we do not climb into a healthy body and just stay there; we go through it, come out the other side into a healthy mind, and in time unite the two into a healthy spirit. This is not to say the spirit cannot develop ahead of both mind and body; often it does, only its progress is unnecessarily impeded. Thus with no regard for the healthful aspects of animal abstinence, we might help the body along in spite of itself, and be vegetarians more for metaphysical motives.

Big fish kill small fish; small people kill big and small fish; and big people kill big fish, small fish, small people, and themselves. Who but the biggest of all big people can hope to restrain any of this killing; and how but by killing can anyone hope to enforce it? As an answer to such questions, vegetarianism embodies religion, as many religions embody vegetarianism. But unlike religious prohibitions, the inspiration for vegetarianism must come from within. One should no more compel another to eat one's food than to be oneself, because one's food becomes oneself. Not everyone is intended to be a vegetarian.

Every human might be identified with an entire species of animal. Indeed, as many varieties of humans may exist as there are distinct mammalian species. Thus, some humans resemble herbivorous chipmunks, deer, or giraffes; others vegetarian hogs, elephants, or hippopotami; still others carnivorous tigers, wolves, or hyenas. As is true in the animal kingdom, most humans eat no flesh at all, or at most once a week. The point is that if many of us are meant to eat as the apes do, some of us are meant to eat as the lions do. But the ratio of American human carnivore to vegetarian is far greater than in the animal kingdom. If more lions than zebras roamed the savannas, the lions eventually would extirpate both the zebras and themselves. In essence such self-destruction is happening to us, as too many predators dwell among us in our brutalized, big cities.

Vegetarianism is a diet that offers a panacea for a long life not just for particular humans, but for the species as a whole. Our sophistry cannot escape the unsleeping and unerring justice of nature. And yet, and yet: humans do differ from animals; animals are governed by natural law, humans by natural law and by free will. Thus each member of the human family resists nature merely in being human. We are humans, different from other animals; and we are individuals, different from other humans. Along with lists of well-known reasons for vegetarianism, some compile lists of well-known vegetarians, presenting that second list as though part of the first. Who should care how many notable people have been vegetarians? That many, great or common, have done something is no reason for another's doing it; surely far more notable people in Western history have been carnivorous. No list of thousands counts as much as the individual plurality of one. Vegetarianism's cause is not in need of credentials, references, or membership lists. The only vegetarian one need know is oneself, as one need know oneself generally.

Minerals are material. Plants are material and alive. Animals are material, alive, and sentient. Higher animals are material, alive, sentient, and mental. Humans are material, alive, sentient, mental, and sentimental. Each evolutionary form incorporates and adds to the form before it. Thus each knows not only itself, but the form before it on the evolutionary scale, and sometimes as much about that form as about itself. A carnivorous animal knows general habits about its victim's life useful in its capture, its life during its final hours. A carnivorous American, however, knows little about the farm animal's life, next to nothing about its final hours just before its death, and nothing about its death.

Vegetarians are not a better sort of people, just a better sort of carnivore; and carnivores are just a better sort of cannibal. On the assumption they would become depositaries of their vanquished enemies' courage and strength, ancient warriors ate the brains, hearts, organs, or sometimes whole bodies of their conquered. In modern times, human animals no longer eat other humans, even their enemies; but other animals are still eaten as though *they* were enemies. The breeds of animals eaten have changed, however. Past centuries fed heavily on wild animals; the primary source now is domasticated (sic) animals, those changed, and chained, by human will.

Still, the universe manifests its order in a way humans who have long lost touch with nature can hardly suspect. We are allotted only a fixed amount of food for our lifetimes: no more, though sometimes less. We also are responsible for the future into which we shall move, sooner or later creating one in which there is no more room to move. Those who eat more than youth's or midlife's share become fat: fat people die younger, having exhausted their allowance early. Flesh eaters every year require six hectares of land to feed a cow with grains and grasses that they might feed themselves with beef, as opposed to lacto-vegetarians who need two hectares to feed a cow grains and grasses that they might feed themselves with milk, as opposed to complete vegetarians who detour the cow altogether and use but half a hectare to feed themselves with grains and grasses. Conservation of soil, air, water, and plant and animal life in general rests most precariously on the conservation of calories.

But more important than the caloric is the karmic debt. Bad enough to kill an animal, it's worse to raise it precisely to be killed. Life in the darkened veal stall or the cramped battery cage is hardly life at all compared to freedom in the meadow or forest. Bad enough to kill an animal, it's worst to eat it. The inherent cholesterol, toxins, uric acid, high bacteria count, general indigestibility, and lack of fiber in the flesh of the animal eaten whose life was aborted in turn shortens the life of the eater animal. "Shortening" is no euphemism for "lard."

Generations ago, when more wilderness remained, eating an animal was not such a malevolent act; wild animals flourished, and fewer humans were around to eat them. In the wild, those animals that survived the first weeks after birth lived longer; natural selection discards the very oldest first, the very youngest second, and all the others third. But factory farming has interfered with nature's designs, and most animals never live past the time they attain full biological growth. The human age equivalent would be filleted at fifteen or sautéed at sixteen. So the debt humans accumulate increases, repaid by shorter healthy lives. The penalties are enforced by technologies: added antibiotics, sodium nitrite and other preservatives, injected artificial hormones, and accumulated insecticides in the bodies of the farm animals. The animals' own hormones, particularly adrenaline, and toxins are secreted, and wastes excreted, at the slaughtering places. The hormones and toxins serve to shorten and sicken the lives of those who serve and eat the flesh. Those who live by the swordfish die by the swordfish.

On evidence as obvious as the omnipresent McDonald's golden arches that rise above the highway like Parsee Towers of Silence, an American carnivore consumes an estimated weight of flesh totaling more than half a steer a year. The steer is rare that is allowed to live longer than two of its potential twenty-two years of life, so a karmic debt of those fifteen to twenty unlived years of a steer life is accumulated. Accumulated by whom? By the steer's unknown mother? By its unborn young? By the factory farmer? By the hot dog vendor on the street? Clearly it is by, more than any other, the carnivore.

Let us imagine a scale in eternity's ledger whereby the worth of each species on the earth, indeed, the worth of the earth, is tabulated. It might reveal that a year of a chicken's life equals a month of a sheep's equals a week of a cow's equals a day of a human's. Based on arbitrary assumptions about this hypothetical golden rule, stolen steer life converts at the exchange rate of one steer week to one human day. Fifteen stolen steer years times fifty-two weeks a year yield 780 weeks of steer life, which in turn equal 780 days of human life—roughly two years. This two year "human-steer" debt corresponds exactly to the human time taken to accumulate it, so each day a person remains a carnivore in his youth represents at the end one less day of good health, or of life altogether.

This method of calculation is the basis of much criminal sentencing, wherein one year of one human life equals one year of another human life (an eye for an eye, a tooth for a tooth): first degree murderers accumulate debts equal to the duration the deceased might otherwise have lived and, assuming murderer and murdered are approximately the same age, as is often the cases of both best friends and worst enemies, the criminals are sentenced to life imprisonment.

Though we are prisoners of our bodies, we have no cause to suffer our incarceration. When just one passion overwhelms the body, it allows easy infiltration of all the rest. The alcoholic and narcotic, the libertine and nicotine, are all habits that combine forces to overcome the body and cause it to fail. Those who seek to create harmony out of a carnivorous diet might as well seek peace out of necromancy. Searching is in itself good, but useless when in the wrong place altogether. Better to save time and not seek it; better to save crime and leave it out. Why indenture our souls with bodies of others? Is not our own enough? Is not our own too much? It's hard enough to be ourselves, we need not try to be cows, pigs, lambs, or chickens.

Certain organs, such as livers and kidneys, filtrate and accumulate food poisons, including insecticides. What these organs do in human bodies they do also in animal bodies: eating the animal body, particularly its liver, gathers not just the human share but also the animal's. If you are what you eat, it is because you are what you do not excrete. No wonder kidneys are often overworked in flesh eaters: they must cleanse not just the bodies of the eaters, but the bodies of all those eaten.

It is difficult to try to know oneself amidst the confusing presence of so many other bodies within our own. When the tongue must taste another's tongue, the stomach digest another's stomach, the blood vessels circulate another's blood, the intestines excrete as feces another's intestines and maybe also feces, who can "know thyself?" Rather, Gnaw Thyself.

Time now to progress from commentary to commitment: presentation of these "problems of nutrition" is hardly justified without one suggestion of solution. Three guidelines exist for choosing our food, keys with which to open the door of our own flowering: *Eat foods as Raw, as Whole, and as Fresh as possible.*

First, concerning *Raw* foods, most vegetables that we customarily cook actually taste better raw, which most of us are too habituated to recognize. Cooking never puts anything in, but only takes much out. Raw plant foods retain all their beneficial enzymes, some of which even assist our digestion of those plants; but the only enzymes flesh contains are the ones we would not want, those which in larger amounts would digest us. When a human eats tongue, who is tasting whom? Food should be eaten raw whenever possible; flesh, however, must be cooked to destroy all its germs.

Second, concerning *Whole* foods, few animals are eaten entirely in one sitting. Six or seven sardines might be swallowed in one sandwich, but two years are needed to consume the equivalent of one beef cow. This is only statistical since most shy away from organs, eating them only when disguised inside intestinal casings and called cold cuts and hot dogs: if these eaters knew they were eating brains and eyes, perhaps their brains would guide them where their eyes had failed. Everything in nature harmonizes both with nature and to itself. The term *natural* applies to those foods that are balanced and that maintain harmony within their consumers, so that they in turn will do so with the whole of nature. Hence natural food store shelves are nearly fleshless, and one in six such shoppers is vegetarian.

Third, concerning *Fresh* foods, dare carnivores consume flesh fresh, blood still pulsating inside bodies? But who objects to an apple just picked from the tree, sap still dripping from the stem? Few carnivores eat truly fresh flesh; they act not as predators, but as scavengers, eating animals killed by others, and killed days or weeks ago. Any alteration of food that occurs in the name of preservation acts only to diminish nutrition. Often this alteration renders the food unrecognizable, and nearly as often this is done purposely; thus, few can discern the lamb from its chops, or the pig from its pork. Flesh is food processed before any human has even seen it: it is recomposed plants hidden behind and inside a decomposed animal.

Those who attempt to know the inner self find that a host of deviations, all inimical to progress, appear out of the unknown, or rather out of their own unknowing. It is a long, hard climb for the body up the mountain of the mind. We need be neither orologists nor mountaineers to know that the very dead weight of animals slung across our shoulders or around our bellies hardly alleviates the strain of the endeavor. The higher the mountain and the longer the climb, the smaller we then see ourselves to be. Not all religious movements or spiritual leaders proscribe carnivorism, but then almost none explicitly demand it either. Those who have gained self-realization can understand how inconsequential all humanity is, and can know that all its actions, good or bad, real or imagined, intended or accidental, amount either to nothing in the face of loftiness, or perhaps to something infinitely small. Such people commit only those actions that reflect that understanding, actions which in themselves can count like Pascal's wager either for good or for nothing, but never for bad. Such an action is vegetarianism.

Big fish kill small fish;
small people kill big and small fish;
and big people kill big fish, small fish,
small people, and themselves.

2.

ASHES TO ASHES, LIFE TO LIFE

I swallow down my food, but the slightest preliminary methodical politico-economical observation of it does not seem to me worthwhile. In this connection the essence of all knowledge is enough for me, the simple rule with which the mother weans the young ones from her teats and sends them out into the world: "Water the ground as much as you can." And in this sentence is not almost everything contained? What has scientific inquiry, ever since our first fathers inaugurated it, of decisive importance to add to this? Mere details, mere details, and how uncertain they are: but this rule will remain as long as we are dogs. It concerns our...food we find on the earth, but the earth needs our water to nourish it and only at that price provides us with our food.

FRANZ KAFKA
"Investigations of a Dog"

BIRTH IS A MIRACLE, death a mystery, but life need be neither misery nor a mistake. Life can be devoted either to soul or to soma, depending in part on whether the mind is three times a day on sesame seeds and sprouts or all the day on aches and pains. Beginning from the mortal wound of birth, for those whose days are measured by diseases alternating between acute and chronic, life is a long disease cured only and slowly by death, the way a jet high in the stratosphere begins its descent many miles before its destination.

"We shall try to achieve *ataraxia*, the undisturbed peace of mind before the turmoil of this world," wrote Luigi Cornaro a half millennium ago, quoting a passage Zeno had written a millennium before. The Greek and Italian were separated by more than just the Adriatic and by more than just a thousand years, but mostly by their two opposing views of actual achievement of *ataraxia*: Zeno, the first Stoic, believed all occurrence was the result of divine will and, therefore, we should accept our fates with calm and without complaint, while Cornaro believed we can take our lives into our hands because we, after all, can take our foods into our hands. Cornaro is our first modem writer on nutrition. What he wrote then is no less true now, just as most current writings on nutrition are no different from and nothing newer than what was written in the first American health food books at the beginning of the twentieth century.

Cornaro's youth and middle age were marked by indulgence in all that wealthy Venice offered, funded by what others had earned. At forty he contracted a near-fatal illness, but through a life of simplicity and moderation regained his health and lived to a ripe one hundred and two. During his last sixty years, the author of *Della Vita Sobria* redirected his efforts to serving the same people upon whom he was previously parasitic. He became an architect and helped to build Venice. Everything gotten must be given back.

Most nutritionists are more akin to mathematicians with tables and charts, and to physicians with tablets and shots, than to metaphysicians. Neither theologians nor moral philosophers equate health with virtue; neither doctors nor nutritionists associate sickness with sin. When one thing precedes another their relationship may either be causation or succession. The American diet seems to lead the way to many diseases, but the diet and the diseases could very well stem from a common ground: perdition. In such cases, disease should be not the concern of doctors, but of priests. Christian Scientists partially agree. Should not the society that promotes the sale of pills, alcohol, tobacco, caffeine, and flesh be as liable for illnesses as the individual who purchases them? Economic systems stand to profit or to lose from an individual's health or illness as much as any one individual. Declines and falls of civilizations are popularly attributed to political or social causes rather than to any nutritional root, but some historians have blamed Rome's fall less to Attila and more to the opium in Romans' smoking pipes and to the lead in their water pipes. Nations, like individual citizens, are born, grow, age, die, and are buried. Death must be accepted, indeed expected, with life. Food, which is life, whether from plants or from animals from plants, perpetuates this process when the dead animal is buried and thereby reprocessed back into the same soil from which originally grew the plants it ate. Everything gotten must be given back.

Earth is the center and the foundation upon which plant life and therefore animal life depend. Plants need animals to replenish the soil just as animals need plants to recycle the air and to convert solar energy into food energy. Modern America's food is deficient not in quantity but in the nutrients that define its quality. If plants are grown tall in it but never tilled back in it, soil becomes depleted until eventually the plants that grow in the soil show paltry growth, and the animals that eat the plants become malnourished.

Ponder small suburban backyard gardens that supply much of a family's vegetables during summer and early fall. Vegetable gardeners' predominant reason for cultivating their yards is concern with supplying their families with fresh produce. Yet, many use chemical fertilizers and chemical insecticides. Others fertilize organically, and rather than toss kitchen scraps into the trash, they compost. Many also compost the weekly clippings from lawns and the yearly foliage from trees. A new generation has emerged whose symbol is the compost heap, not the garbage heap. But one crucial link in nature's cycle is ignored: regenerating into the garden our very bodies. Instead, our families conceal our remains far away in cemeteries relegated to the most desolate corners of society, as though garbage in some dump. Some of us even plot our escapes beforehand, prepaying for our gravesites, visiting them before our deaths, like little pharaohs devoting their lives to the construction of their pyramids. Finally, we die, at last we can return to that from which we came; but instead our bodies are stuffed into airtight coffins into which the sands of time do not trickle for hundreds of years. Or some of us are cremated, which affords others the opportunity to toss our ashes to the wind, or to return our ashes to the ground. Ashes of some of the deceased, however, are locked into urns. D. H. Lawrence's wife mixed his ashes into a two-ton block of cement. All men are not cremated equal.

In contrast, George Bernard Shaw wished his ashes to be scattered in his garden, and suggested enacting a law that a tree be planted for anyone who dies. Those whose bodies are buried in the simplest boxes of pine immediately inherit the earth by fertilizing lawns; but in a hundred years, when their names are forgotten by their descendents and eroded off their tombstones, those lawns just might become farms or forests. Meanwhile, we dig our own graves, ignoring the cosmic fact that everything gotten must be given back.

Plants, animals, and humans are isogenous, and thus plants nourish animals and humans, who in turn fertilize plants. The question "What is the purpose of human existence?" is sometimes answered: "To raise children." If the purpose of our parents' lives was to give birth to us and ours is to give birth to their grandchildren, then the purpose of our parents' deaths is to nourish us and of ours to nourish their grandchildren. The answer really is: "To raise plants."

Thus, the problem of what to eat could be solved solely by knowing what food would cause our bodies to more adequately replenish the earth, both through the little parts of ourselves we leave behind every day and the lump sum we leave when we pass over to the other side of life. We, of course, could be eaten by carnivores, but carnivores also return to the soil, and so would we, though indirectly. Since the carnivore who eats other carnivores is the exception rather than the rule, this precludes our never returning to the soil by being fed to our children, unless we were vegetarians. But what vegetarians would raise their children as carnivores? What vegetarians would feed their children others' children?

We might nourish future generations more quickly and more directly by being buried at the trunk of a tree. We grow on fruits, fruits grow on trees, trees grow on us. One devoted son visits the apple tree which grows over his father's grave each fall, and gathers the apples which have fallen to the ground. The following week he drinks and eats nothing but the juice from those apples, and does little else but write poetry. That poetry he dedicates to his father, hoping that completion will be reached through light which death would not permit through life.

Primitive humans probably survived larger predators since a carnivore's flesh is seldom as sweet nor as savory as an herbivore's. The poet could not eat his father—that would have been very hard for him to have gotten down—but he can easily eat from the tree from which his father once ate and which now consumes his father. He could also eat the squirrel that eats from the tree, but that places him twice removed from his father. Although the very closest he could get to his father would be to join him in the world of the dead, as long as the poet remains in the world of the living then the closest he can get is by eating the apples. Now it must be remembered that he is a poet and rarely speaks literally or historically, but usually metaphorically and allegorically, always tropologically, and in this case anagogically: the father is no father at all, but is the mother, Mother Earth.

Egoism, the opposite of Earth, is our deepest-rooted tendency and separates our individual goals from those which Mother Earth had intended. We act in the interest of Earth only when laboring under the delusion that these actions benefit only ourselves. Earth, understanding more than any individual, dupes us into serving her while we, who rarely understand ourselves and barely ever more than that, believe all along we are motivated by purely personal reasons. "Each false feeling produces the absolute certainty of having it," wrote Pier Paolo Pasolini, in a poem titled "A Desperate Vitality." "My false feeling was that of health." Our entire purpose in relation to plants is to fertilize them. Thus Earth deludes us into believing we seek health for selfish effects when, in fact, it is for the sake of more consistent and more frequent bowel movements, that is, recyclable fertilizer. Those who are embarrassed or simply bewildered by these scatological matters demonstrate their conditioning by a society that conceals the functions of the bathroom as much as of the slaughterhouse, a society that after all is on the side of Egoism, not of Earth.

Though Earth can delude us, we can never defraud Earth; to try to do so is to dupe ourselves out of our health, or to dupe our grandchildren out of theirs, though our health is itself a delusion. If we continue to defecate (literally) into rivers rather than onto earth, the Earth will defecate (figuratively) on us. We can better prepare ourselves to nourish our fateful apple tree more immediately by being nourished by it and by other apple trees, on account of the laxative effect of fruit. Ponder a ripe apple and a dead squirrel side by side on the ground, the apple fallen from its limb, the squirrel fallen from its life. As they both begin to decay, the apple decomposes beyond recognition early in winter before the first snow, while the squirrel's body may remain identifiable even after the last snow has melted under the spring sun, and its bones might last many more months before being gnawed by rodents other than other squirrels. Fruit requires an hour to be digested in the stomach, but flesh four or more; similarly, fruit requires less time than flesh to decompose into earth. So maybe, just maybe, a lean human body nourished largely from fruit decomposes more quickly than a fatty one nourished from flesh. In regards to karma, not only must the carnivore's body decompose, but of all its consumed bodies lurking within its own must decompose, too.

Our whole role in this cycle is not merely a destiny to die, but to live until we die, and while we live to excrete as much fertile feces as possible. Merely eating a lot does not mean eating wisely, especially if it causes obesity, which induces improper digestion and irregular bowel movements and constipation.

Regular bowel movements manifest good health, because what is good for Earth is good for ego. Thus Kafka's mother dog instructs her young puppies: "Water the ground as much as you can." (Anyone who reads Kafka's *Investigations of a Dog* alongside Dostoyevsky's *Notes from the Underground,* and Kafka's *The Burrow* alongside Defoe's *Robinson Crusoe,* will understand the basis for Kafka's vegetarianism.) This duty to Earth explains dogs' instinct to water at the trunks of trees, to return to Earth what they have taken from her as directly and as immediately as possible, particularly because of their carnivorism. "Instinct" explains what humans cannot explain in animals, what humans long ago have forgotten and never again shall recall.

As mostly urbanites like our predecessors the cave-dwellers, we have shed instinct and have adapted to an unnatural environment. If we are the highest form of animal life, and if we are to eat plants, these should be from the highest forms of plant life, namely fruits and nuts from trees. But instead most of us eat pizza and burgers, consequent of eating what is local to our environment dominated by pizza parlors and fast food joints. Fire hydrants memorialize where trees once grew, and our dogs, too, have adapted to our environment.

Conclusions may be reached either by deduction or by observation. Observation of our city streets relates to us differences between two diets by what two fellow mammals leave behind them: much dog feces everywhere, despite poop scoop laws, and occasional horse feces around parks. The former forces ever wary pedestrians to detour from their intended paths and to hold their noses, while the latter may even attract our interest because of its inoffensive earthy odor. Horses eat oats; dogs eat horses.

Ego echoes Earth just as digestion echoes decomposition and fertilization. Consider also the protein combination needed to supply the human body with balanced essential amino acids: one-part legume to three-parts grain, nut or seed; or expressed equally, one-part legume to one-part grain to one-part nut to one-part seed. Now consider the crop rotation necessary to prevent soil depletion: one year of legumes alternated with three years of grains or seeds or other vegetables. Hence combination echoes rotation.

Has enough been said, or too much? Thought without reflection leads nowhere. We should take a breather to ponder whether the content of this chapter has approached somewhat closer to the truth than where it began. During such respites, the ancients sought oracles by sorting through the feces of animals.

Even if in apparent opposition like acid and alkaline, sodium and potassium, or yin and yang, two diets might combine well together, throw light on one another, and complement each other as do soy and oats on the breakfast table, or red and green on the color wheel. A lazy mind would grasp only where they differ, an alert mind also where they agree. To better evaluate vegetarianism we would do well to contemplate carnivorism. But why look up close at what even from a distance stinks of blood and gore? Like attracts like, but that which reeks repels everything, except for flies and their maggots. Those who smoke tobacco have every right to poison themselves in whatever they wish, but no right to lure others into their mire. Just as smokers are separated from non-smokers in public places, someday so will be carnivores from non-carnivores in restaurants and dining halls. To those with nasal passages as clear as their conscience, the smell of burning flesh is far more nauseating than burning tobacco.

"What's for supper?" is a short question with a long history of many answers. Food for thought about food has been as diverse as Western philosophies, world religions, social dogmas, and political platforms. While no one *must* reason or believe or conform or vote, everyone must eat. So what's for supper, Mom? In the Arctic, the answer is codfish or the flesh of a walrus; in Tahiti, breadfruit or the flesh of a coconut. Climates differ, local foods differ, and what is suitable to each environment differs. The body temperature of a living walrus is warmer than the Arctic snow, so Eskimos eat walrus to keep themselves warm; a growing fruit is cooler than the tropical winds blowing through its tree's branches, so Polynesians eat fruit to keep themselves cool. Ethnic origins also affect dietary needs. In America, land of the mongrel, a Chinese American in Chinatown thrives on a diet different from an Italian American in Little Italy, though they both live on Mott Street in downtown Manhattan.

We foolishly believe that people can be summarized in a single sentence, so when first introduced, we query their livelihood, or if male their age, or if New Age their astro sign, or if old age enough to read novels their favorite writer, or if young enough to care about it their computer platform, or their political party's platform, or their favorite genre of music, or if Caucasian their favorite ethnic foods...or if vegetarian their blacklisted forbidden foods. Or we might not ask but might guess their ethnic origin. Mainland and menu are the same; people spring from their foods that spring from their soils. In the end, we are asking from what earth their bodies had come, and wondering into what earth their bodies shall return.

Our choice is between eating obediently what a sick society tells us to eat, or wisely what the eternal Earth wants us to eat. After consciously guiding ourselves to eat only real food, eventually we will desire only that which now nourishes us, and that later nourishes the Earth. But until we ascend to that stage, we might wonder, as did a young carnivorous king, just what single book on vegetarian nutrition to read. The young king had several wise men and wiser women at his command, so he instructed them to write a single treatise on the theory and practice of vegetarian nutrition, one addressing carnivores such as he. The result was a book that provided an easy transition by not demanding much and by not telling the whole truth, but only the germ. The king was clearly instructed what to do and how to do it, with many formulas and recipes. The wise men and women assumed the collective pseudonym of Frances M. Lappé, and chose for their book the title *Diet for a Small Planet*.

It had taken ten years to write; none of the wise men or women had retired or died, so the still youthful king sent them away again. This time he asked them to simplify the menu, to exclude sea animals entirely, and to de-emphasize protein in general and milk and eggs in particular. The king himself had gained some insight and could point the way. For another ten years the men and women pondered and labored. Like canaries in mine shafts, they examined their own health as measures of the Earth's. Transcending Twinkies and renouncing Baskin-Robbins ice cream, they called themselves John Robbins and researched a thicker book, titled *Diet for a New America*.

The king's health remained fine, but able to afford it he sought more. He again sent the wise men and women away, this time for forty years in the desert, to prepare a book not just about nourishing the body but also about nurturing the soul. After long study, the wise ones came to understand that total health is assured not just from proper food, but from strenuous exercise, moderate sunlight, fresh air, deep sleep, tranquil rest, and the rest of many practices based both in New Age hocus-pocus and in Old World esoteric exotica. Along with their raw food vegan diet, they fasted periodically and practiced what the West calls deep breathing and visualization, which the East calls yoga and meditation. Simplifying principles of Natural Hygiene in order to be understood by millions of readers, they figured to earn themselves millions of dollars. Bridging gender gaps, they used the first names Harvey and Marilyn. Writing for posterity, they used the durable last name Diamond. Still healthy, now wealthy, and always wise, the joint authors could live as they saw fit. So they called their book *Fit for Life II: Living Health.*

During forty years of wandering in the desert, the old wise men and older wiser women continued their total vegetarian diets and continued their totally good health, though some now limped with canes or crutches. They returned to the king to bestow upon him their latest book. During that same time, however, the king had abandoned proper diet, blaming the rigors of royalty for his spiritual lassitude. In fact, the new book was useless to him, because he no longer could see to read it. So he instructed his entourage to retreat again to the desert and to return only after condensing all vegetarian nutritional knowledge into one sentence.

For forty days and forty nights the wise ones fasted. After much contemplation and deliberation they issued their ultimate edict, and after less deliberation all but one decided to make their final home there in the desert. Only one solitary wise man returned to the king. The old king was bedridden, so the one wise man bent down and spoke softly into the old king's ear: "We grow on fruits, fruits grow on trees, trees grow on us: everything gotten must be given back."

He then broke his forty day fast on grapes, and while he ate, the king looked on. The king made some feeble gestures signifying that he had not understood what was spoken, for the elderly king was now nearly deaf, dumb, and blind. So the wise man knelt down and placed in the king's sweaty hand a single grape. The king held it in his palm like a blind father embracing his prodigal son. He then understood everything, inhaled one last smell of the sweet air, and passed over into the other side of life. The wise man buried him in a nearby vineyard, amid grapevines for which the king's body soon would provide fertilizer.

Nutrition is not an ever-expanding realm of research about which seekers must keep informed of recent developments: the latest weight-loss fad, the newest miracle vitamin discovery, the most innovative and fraudulent aging preventative measure. Rather, it diminishes to simpler and simpler irrefutable laws. The entire question of what to eat could be condensed to the answer of a single grape, which encompasses complexity itself.

The progress of human civilization appears to be unraveling backwards: that is, from the simple to the complex. Our modern economies revolve around our inability to do things for ourselves, and thus our dependence on others. Humans are strange creatures who eat animals but rarely eat what they kill. A mouse heard one night within a wall will find traps set in a room corner in the morning; but few humans kill in the morning the cow they intend to eat for supper. Neither killing nor

eating animals is to be condoned, but the one vice seems to device the other when done together. The sight, sound, smell, and
certainty of death attracts even the cowardly, particularly if the
death of a bitter enemy or a convicted criminal. Soldiers more
willingly may risk their lives in battle when prospects favor the
enemy's defeat. In the same vein, public hangings were once
as great a social event as our summer Sunday church chicken
barbecues. The basic attraction for flesh foods is contained in
the taste of blood, but also in the sense of security of its being
someone else's. If nations " ...shall beat their swords into
plowshares, and their spears into pruning hooks" (Isaiah 2:4),
all swords, not just weapons of warfare, must be transformed:
rather than possess both butcher knives and plowshares, we
need keep only the latter. Yet we occupy ourselves not with
plowshares, swords, or knives, but with shopping carts. Unlike
primitive hunters who risked their lives killing animals, Diana
housewives of the supermarket hunt risk theirs eating them.

Nature's laws, which abhor superfluities as much as vacu-
ums, command simplicity, and this means the simplest diet.
But just as two things similar are not the same, no two people
find the same things simple. Thus vegetarianism varies from
mere omission of flesh to near-fruitarianism. Whatever way
is followed, so long as it is accompanied by vitamin pills, the
way is not simple enough; any need for pills is an indication
of the inadequacy of the diet. They are a medicine to be taken
for as long as disease or its risk persists, but no longer than
needed and as little as possible. Mega-doses are contradictory
to their whole aim: no great talent or thought is necessary to
take as much as possible, the only limiting factor being one's
purse. However, if a vitamin is used as medicine, the supplicant need not falsify the highest standards nor pander to the

lowest. Vitamins are needed to assimilate the protein and minerals in food, which is difficult to accomplish by the body that suffers from malnourishment due in part to lack of vitamins. Pills can actually be crucial for a smooth transition from fake foods to real foods, from the nugatory to the natural.

Ours is an age of convenience typified by pills and potions, and an age of impatience exemplified by cars and trucks that rush to red lights and speed to stop signs. Not thankful for having a banana from thousands of miles away, most mix ingratitude with impatience by rarely eating it fully ripened when its skin is black or brown. Or, realizing that a yellow or green banana is unripe, but unwilling to wait for a week, some bake or fry it. A pot of whole wheat berries simmered for hours is more digestible than one quickly boiled for half an hour, and more nourishing than instant farina to which boiled water is added in the breakfast bowl. Imagine the greater value of a seven-day shoot of wheat grass! Patience being the first criterion for indoor sprouting, eventually patience grows with the sprouts, and we can pass our days sitting on the front porch watching the grass grow.

Patience also is necessary for dietary transitions. The slower the transition, the more stable the result. As in love, impatience forms only loose bonds to the ideal to which we are committed. Typical beginnings lead to typical ends, or to total catastrophe. This happened to an aged man who had spent all his life searching for the fountain of youth. One day he found it and, forgetting his age, his arthritis, and his obesity, he jumped right in—and drowned. But even through error we gain some access to a higher ideal; so long as we are ahead of our time, we can afford to go slowly. In chewing food, the one who chews slowly, wins. Likewise in choosing foods.

A life contains hardly time enough to know everything about ourselves or everything about nutrition, but a few months is sufficient to know for ourselves all we need to know about nutrition. The months, however, should not be contiguous, but separated by years. Ten years to assure a smooth transition from cooked carnivorism to raw vegetarianism is not long compared to the thousands taken the other way around. Eleven basic steps might be outlined, one for each year, not all of which need be done, nor one by one.

The foothold from which our whole discussion springs is exemplified by sirloin steak, supplemented by dad's backyard barbecued hot dogs and mom's homemade apple pies. Less loved children learn to settle for Pop Tarts and Big Macs. Actually Big Macs can be credited with transforming many children into vegetarians. But probably the one meal most responsible for such transformations is Thanksgiving, when the family gathers around the excavated body of a dead turkey. At such Thanksgiving dinners, most families do little thanking, do mostly getting, while turkeys do all the giving.

> 'Twas the night before Thanksgiving,
> when all through the pantry,
> Not a creature was stirring,
> Least of all the dead turkey.

At *Step One*, the book addressed directly to our vast American populace is the groundbreaking *Diet for a Small Planet*. But its substitution of mammals and birds with fish, of meat with milk, is comparable to switching from white sugar to raw sugar, from high-tar cigarettes to low. A second step is lacking, indeed begging; cutting out merely white meat effects little or no improvement in one's health. The other two white staples of white America's diet, namely white flour and white sugar, also must be trashed. Such vegetarianism, whose adherents are seldom healthier than before, is the type which has most to gain from perusal into further sources.

At *Step Two* we learn what is so unhealthful about white foods, why to eat produce fresh, how little protein we really need, indeed how few foods we really need. At this stage, the writings about diet by health guru Andrew Weil are worthy of examination. Fish and sea animals, however, are still eaten. Then one day, while dining on lobster, we hear the story of the red crustacean mercilessly dropped into boiling water, struggling afloat until sinking into oblivion, becoming the soup of suffering in our spoons, the monster in our mouths, the beast in our bellies.

Thus at *Step Three* the animals of the sea join ranks with those of the land, and all are left better safe than quarry. Until this step, we were "proto-vegetarians," or "almost vegetarians," or "tentative vegetarians." Now we are lacto-ovo-vegetarians. Hurray, we have arrived; or maybe not.

At *Step Four* we come to realize that dairy in the diet causes as much mucus to flow from one's nose as blood from the calf's neck: so we grow up, and wean from Mother Cow. *Step Five*, when we stay away from eggs the chickens lay away, occurs as often before Step Four as after, and usually right along with it. Although many macrobiotics eat sea animals, Steps Four and Five conform to macrobiotic principles; so here any of Michio Kushi's writings are valuable. Essentially a gourmet's guide to nutrition as well as to philosophy, macrobiotics has its limitations. Its followers soon tire of chopping and frying and boiling and baking. Objections also arise regarding its emphasis on cooked grains and beans to the exclusion of fresh fruits, its salting everything despite the plentiful inclusion of sea vegetables, its fresh vegetables cooked to the consistency of canned vegetables, and the devotion of a large part of the literature to the cure of ailments that no one is supposed to contract.

So *Step Six* slowly supersedes Five: fresh fruits become a main staple, vegetables are eaten only raw, salt is excluded altogether, and the few ailments about which we might complain are ameliorated simply with fasting. All this is basically the regimen of Paul Bragg's writings, the dietetics of joy, as demonstrated by his infectious smile, the only infection he may ever have contracted, and by his picture of health even his nineties. (Was he really writing a book entitled *I Challenge Death* when, at the age of ninety-five, he died?)

With *Step Seven* the health food store and produce market supersede the supermarket, where we now might go only for bathroom and kitchen supplies. The kitchen itself becomes limited in use and larger in space, with the removal of the stove and oven. We learn to turn off the gas, which was a sort of laughing gas, for the laugh was on us. We even might imitate Johnny Appleseed and wear pots on our heads: that would be our only remaining use for them. By this time, ninety-five percent of our food is raw, that is, one cooked meal a week. This step puts us on the path of Natural Hygiene, a very sterile name for a very natural diet. Its best of many writers is Herbert Shelton. We learn not only what to eat, but when to eat, what to eat together, and when not to eat altogether. Fresh fruits eaten with seeds or nuts are good, but eaten alone are better; fresh vegetables eaten alone are good, but eaten with nuts or seeds are better; fruits and vegetables are better not eaten together; and best of all are those days when we eat nothing at all.

A modified form of fruitarianism evolves at *Step Eight.*
Actually this includes nuts and seeds from the health food store,
and sprouts and grasses from our own windowsill gardens.
Fruitarianism in its broadest sense does not entail eating only
fruits, but rather the selected substitution of foods that fall
from the plant for those that are the plants themselves. Thus
apples and berries are "fruit-fruits"; almonds and Brazils are
"nut-fruits"; sesame and sunflower are "seed-fruits"; and pep-
pers and pumpkins are "vegetable-fruits." While the tomato is
a "fruit," the potato is not. And sprouts, not quite a vegetable
but only a short time ago a seed or a bean or a nut, are the
best of both worlds. There is no one perfect food, but just as
the egg is most nearly perfect for the carnivore, the fruit and
the sprout are for the vegetarian. Yet we are not talking about
perfection, nor even about how to reach perfection; all we
are discussing is how to reach. This diet with emphasis upon
sprouts is articulated by several eloquent speakers and writers; among them are Viktoras Kulvinskas, Gabriel Cousens,
and Brian Clement. The healthier vegetarians are those of us
whose diets rest somewhere along Steps Six, Seven, and Eight;
these are the steps about which more detailed discourse can be
found elsewhere in this book (chapters 3 and 8).

And then, *Step Nine,* "fruit-fruitarianism." Many scientific vegetarians denigrate this with even more zeal than carnivorism, but as long as we do not mistake dream for reality,
why can't we dream? After all, people dreamed for thousands
of years about landing on the moon before actually achieving
the feat. Perhaps we should dream next about landing on the
sun. Given the right raw material, a pure body, just maybe,
may be able to manufacture everything it needs, protein and
B12 included. Fruit may be that right raw material, but no

one is sure what is a pure body, or if it is any more possible today to mold a pure body than to breathe pure air. Arnold Ehret's writings on "fruit-fruitarianism" instruct that one way to maintain a pure body is through fasting. (Ehret himself might have been the model for Kafka's *Hunger Artist*.) Ehret provides much food for thought, but mostly only for thought, not for eating.

No one need dream to get this far. There are even times when we may need to retreat to old treats, the way a car stuck in the mud must first drive in reverse before further attempting to go forward. So long as we progress slowly enough to know where our particular bodies work best, to know where to turn back if everything doesn't feel fine and to know our bodily functions well enough to recognize when something has gone wrong, then, like Zeno's approach to the wall which is never reached but gets ever closer, we might limit even the variety of fruit. No one reaches any stage of finality in life except by dying.

If we dare dream, *Step Ten* awaits, the number of completion and perfection according to Pythagorean numerology. We might eat only two meals a day and only two different daily fruits, one for each meal. Consider the apple and the banana, our least expensive and most widely available fruits. Next we might choose between the apple and the banana, and if we live in a non-tropical zone, the apple might suffice. Unlike the banana, it flourishes in our own northerly climates and possesses no wasteful skin to throw away. Its dozen seeds provide protein, its one or two leaves attached to the stem some chlorophyll. The apple might epitomize *Step Eleven*, the itemizer of the ideal, and humanity's first food from the Fall could become its last before the return of Paradise.

It is no coincidence that the chief cause of death in the domasticated [sic] animal world is slaughter, while in the human world it is starvation. While one half of the human world diets, the other half dies. As terrible as all the animal lives wasted are all the human lives lost or led astray. The goal is not just to reduce desire for any particular food, or for all foods, but to reduce all desires. The person obsessed by ten desires who satisfies five of them is only half as happy as, not five times happier than, the person who has just one desire and fully satisfies that.

So what if we desire only apples? That is still a desire that nags for satisfaction. So we could aim straight for Step Twenty-Two, the number of expansion and ascension, the Master Number, though only in a material sense; we might transcend food altogether. Dust collects over everything we eat, until eventually it is all we eat. Ultimately we would reach down into the ground, pull up a handful of earth, and eat it: to eat what we will become. Another way of saying that someone died is: "He bit the dust."

"How much land does a man need?" asked Tolstoy in a short story by that name. The answer: "About six feet by two."

3.

LETTER TO A YOUNG VEGETARIAN
A POSTPRANDIAL PASTICCIO

> SOCRATES: *So the man in training ought to regulate his*
> *actions and exercises and eating and drinking by the*
> *judgment of his instructor, who has expert knowl-*
> *edge, rather than by the opinions of the rest of the*
> *public.... Now if he disobeys the one man and dis-*
> *regards his opinion and commendations, and pays*
> *attention to the advice of many who have no expert*
> *knowledge, surely he will suffer some bad effect....*
> *And what is this bad effect? Where is it produced? I*
> *mean, in what part of the disobedient person?*
> CRITO: *His body, obviously; that is what suffers....*
> SOCRATES: *Then consider the next step. There is a part of*
> *us which is improved by healthy actions and ruined*
> *by unhealthy ones. If we spoil it by taking the advice*
> *of non-experts, will life be worth living when this*
> *part is once ruined? The part I mean is the body....*
> *Well, is life worth living with a body which is worn*
> *out and ruined in health?*
> CRITO: *Certainly not.*
>
> PLATO
> *Crito,* 47

WHAT WE ARE GOING to engage in now is strictly straight
talk, as two good friends from far away and long ago
do in an exchange of letters. The following letter is quite real,
and the reply equally real; but for the sake of argument let

us pretend they are imaginary. On the one hand, we could outline some nutritional advice to apply to everyone, though forsaking our own rather narrow views; on the other hand, we could forget everyone entirely and just speak of what is right for ourselves alone. Let us endeavor to draw our line somewhere near the median of the two menus, with no claim to finality and, we hope, no suggestion of arbitrariness. And let us remember that anything written here can as well be found elsewhere in a hundred other books and a thousand magazines and ten thousand newspapers and a hundred thousand websites.

Dear Mark,

I am interested in a raw food diet without the use of eggs, milk, dairy, fish, fowl or meat. Also, I don't want to eat any food that needs to be blenderized or extensively refrigerated. (I intend to only temporarily use a refrigerator for greens until I can grow plants in a greenhouse or in pots.)

I am looking for specific advice. I've read books that say only, for example, that one can get calcium from sesame seeds, but neglect to say exactly how much to eat for my age, height, and weight.

I am 22 years old, 166 cm. and weigh 55 kg. My questions are:

1) How do I get enough protein? How much of which foods?
2) Calcium. How much of which foods per day?
3) Iron. How much of which foods per day?
4) Iodine. How much of which foods per day? (I don't want to use salt.)
5) B12. Is nutritional yeast really healthful or necessary? Other foods?

6) Is there an alternative to wheat germ?
7) Are supplements necessary?
8) Any other advice about a raw food diet would be appreciated.

I hope you can advise me. Also, will you list any qualifications you might have?

> Peace and peas,
> Marge

Dear Margie,

No one can give you specific advice. You tell your physical characteristics, but what about your nationality and mentality, climate and housemate, altitude and attitude, disposition and occupation, recreation and aspiration? As great a difference exists between the minds of a genius and a fool as between a monkey and a mollusk. Likewise between their bodies. Hippocrates called the human being "That infinitely variable organism without which human disease is impossible." Everyone of different cultural and chromosomal heritage has different nutritional needs. Furthermore, two identical twins leading different lives, and if male, marrying different wives, consequently eat, and need to eat, different foods.

An office worker under a fluorescent lamp needs more vitamin A, an urbanite among automobile exhaust more C, a northerner always indoors or in shade more D, a neurotic under stress extra Bs, etc. The science of nutrition speaks for all humans and completely forsakes the individual. For this reason, "% Daily Value" listed on foods should be ignored. No book can accurately provide the specific information you seek. Only you know when you are hungry, and only you know when you are full. Only you know what foods you like, which if your body is relatively cleansed is also what is good for you. And only you know what foods you dislike, about which one hopes your body is guiding you correctly. The question might be how to assure a cleansed body. The fast way is to fast. The slow and sure way is the raw, or mostly raw, vegetarian diet.

The eater is one variable, the eaten another. Sunlight, soil, water, and seed all vary; so, therefore, do vitamin and mineral contents. Storage further alters everything: an orange eaten right off the tree in Florida has more than twice the vitamin C as another orange off the same branch eaten two months later in Canada. Let us say only that more C is found in an orange than an apple, so if you seek a lot of C eat more oranges than apples. Be suspicious of any table or chart that tells how much C you need or how much more C is in an orange than an apple. The most we can say is: "Eat apples and oranges."

Weigh the first set of variables concerning who is eating on one pan, and the second set concerning what is eaten on the other. If you can balance the scales and read the measurement, your vision is sharper than mine. Faith in absolute uniformity can lead to pill popping: a person reads on a label that so-and-so pill supplies 500 mgs of C, reads in a book that so-and-so person needs 1,000 mgs, and puts 500 and 500 together to get a person who pops two pills a day for the prevention of colds, who increases to four at the first sign of a cold, who increases to ten a day during a cold, and who somehow neglects to consider the cause of the cold.

You've given the example of calcium from sesame seeds. I would no sooner count each milligram of calcium than each seed of sesame.

1. *How do I get enough protein?*
How much of which foods?

In the 1950s, some sources said we needed one hundred grams of protein per day; in the 1960s, eighty grams; now sixty, or one gram daily for every kilogram of body weight. If the countdown continues, in twenty years they'll be telling us twenty grams. If you eat raw, and if you count, perhaps all you need is twenty; but this measurement depends on who you are. And when eating raw, you needn't be too concerned about complementing incomplete proteins because though in small amounts complete protein is found in green leafy vegetables and sprouts, and because the incomplete protein of nuts and seeds will most likely be combined with beans into complete ones. Keep in mind the food-combining laws, and eat nuts and seeds with vegetables. Better still, sprout seeds, grains, and beans *into* vegetables. It is hardly mere chance that general laws for food combining enforce those specifically for protein combining.

While no salad can be considered a reliable quantitative source of protein when served meagerly as a side dish to steak and potatoes, enough can be found when the whole meal is a large bowl of greens. Unsprouted seeds and nuts are nearly complete, particularly sesame and almonds; you might get along if all you ate were either of these. But we are not talking about eating one protein food only. Incidentally, mixed nuts with peanuts (which are peas, not nuts) are cheaper but more complete in protein than mixtures without. But eat the nuts raw and unsalted: roasting and frying destroy the high-quality nut oils, while the cooking oils in which nuts are "roasted" (really fried) are usually motor grade. Salt inhibits the digestion of anything eaten with it, and particularly of oils.

Some find raw and unsalted nuts already difficult to digest. All nuts taste better, are chewed more easily, and are digested more efficiently if soaked for a day. Or soak them for half a day, and germinate them a day. If they are eaten dry, chew each at least thirty-two times, once for each tooth. You can grind nuts and seeds in a blender one cup at a time and add water to make a paste. If you add the soak water from a previous batch that sat in a warm place for a day, and set aside that mixture for another day, you will have fermented the paste into cheese if the batch is thick or into yogurt if it is thin. My favorite is almond, then sunflower. Add kelp and other herb seasonings to what you plan to eat with vegetables, and add fennel, anise, or caraway to those to be eaten with fruits.

Nut milks are quick if not easy preparations. First, grind the dry nuts in the blender, then add a much larger proportion of fruit juice or water, then perhaps a banana. Of course, an objection to blenders is well founded because the heat generated by the blade mildly "cooks" whatever it is blending or grinding. But seeds such as sesame, chia, flax, and psyllium usually pass through the digestive system whole, no matter how much they are chewed, unless they are ground. Those three latter seeds gel into thick shakes when mixed with juice, and into delicious puddings when mixed with whipped fruits such as soaked apricots, dates, or figs.

No discussion of protein is complete without mention of brewer's or nutritional yeast. Yeast is ever so slightly deficient in the essential amino acid methionine, so eat one or two Brazil nuts with it. In fact, many otherwise complete protein foods are ever so slightly deficient in methionine; just keep in mind that Brazil nuts are the highest source.

2. *Calcium. How much of which foods per day?*

You've already spoken of sesame seeds, often touted as high in calcium, though in reality not especially. You may not be aware of the controversy over oxalic acid in their hulls: some say it combines with calcium into an indigestible compound. But a reason to eat those with hulls is that is how they come whole, and so they stay fresher far longer. If not specifically stated as mechanically hulled, de-hulling processes can be chemical, in which case a caustic chemical residue may remain. As with spinach, the trouble with oxalic acid probably occurs when the seed and its hull are heated.

In the raw diet, the foods high in protein are also high in calcium: seeds, nuts, and green leaves. From where do cows get their calcium? Green leaves. The darker the green, the better. Thus the typical American cuisine rests its plastic, gassed tomatoes atop a leafy bed of greens so light as to appear almost white: iceberg lettuce. But even when cooked, kale and collards cup-for-cup contain as much or more calcium than cow's milk. And anyway, pasteurization and homogenization render much of milk's calcium indigestible.

3. *Iron. How much of which foods per day?*

Iron-rich foods are the same foods noted for protein and for calcium. You should see a pattern emerging. Pumpkin seeds are an incredibly rich source of iron, and plenty is found in fruits, particularly the variety that dry readily, whether eaten dry or fresh. Drying is the least detrimental of all preservative processes, but it is still important to restore all dried fruits to their original consistency by soaking. Digestion is improved; and since dried fruit sticks to the teeth with greater tenacity than honey, the one potential cause of cavities in a raw food diet will be reduced by soaking. Honey-dipped fruit, really sugar and honey, eaten dry is worst of all.

If you have to settle for sulfured fruits, throw out the soak water after half an hour and cover the fruit in water again. Under all other circumstances, drink the soak water; it's juice. About juices: drink those freshly squeezed if you wish to drink them at all, though your teeth are efficient juicers, too. Juices in bottles and cartons are all pasteurized. Frozen concentrates are condensed in ways other than evaporation, so they are a smaller form of the same old non-food. Health food stores carry unpasteurized whole frozen juices. This juice tastes almost as good as fresh; as though indeed fresh, once defrosted it quickly ferments. But the difference is this: something fresh ferments, while once cooked it turns rotten. Food must first be good before it can become bad; those which rarely turn bad were probably never good.

4. Iodine. How much of which foods per day? (I don't want to use salt.)

An inorganic mineral no more fit for human consumption than a handful of soil, salt found its way into our diet from its use as a preservative of flesh. Everyone needs sodium and iodine, but no one needs salt. You get ample sodium in earth vegetables, particularly carrots, celery and beets, and plenty of iodine in sea vegetables, especially kelp, in whole form called by its Japanese name, kombu. As they are marketed already cooked, hiziki and arame need only be soaked half an hour. Wakame usually needs further cooking. Dulse need not be cooked, and even soaking is optional. When discussing sea vegetables, we are not talking merely about iodine, but about every trace mineral from the sea. Sea salt has some traces of other minerals, too, but is still mostly sodium chloride. The difference between sea salt and earth salt is like that between raw sugar and white sugar: not much of a difference. Use kelp in place of salt; though heat-dried, its benefits outweigh its single pinch of unworthiness. Buy it by the pound, not the shaker. Mix one-part kelp to one-part dried parsley, dried basil, crushed sesame, etc. This herbal mixture goes well with avocados or vegetable salads.

5. B12. Is nutritional yeast really healthful or necessary? Other foods?

The question most often asked of complete vegetarians is "Where do you get your protein?" The next most frequent question is "What about vitamin B12?" The nutritional rallying cry for complete vegetarianism may either stand or fall on this issue. Conventional carnivorous nutritionists warn that abstinence from flesh, milk, and eggs is as sure a cause of pernicious anemia as indulgence in tobacco is of cancer; yet mothers will react with greater horror on learning that their children have stopped drinking milk and eating eggs than that they had started smoking cigarettes. In fact, the vegetarian who would develop B12-deficiency anemia probably eats very poorly and probably smokes cigarettes. George Bernard Shaw, who ate dairy products, nevertheless suffered from iron-deficiency anemia late in his life; but if we judge from the sweetened crap in the recipe book written by his cook, he deserved his disease. Over-processed white foods and overcooked carbohydrates will lead to disability for anyone, and especially someone past an age when most people had already died.

Evidence suggests that millennia before our forebears ate flesh, they produced B12 in their intestines where it could be assimilated, the way most herbivores do today. Our bodies had to be cleansed to foster intestinal growth of beneficial bacteria, the same strain now used to produce the vitamin in mold cultures for manufacture into pills. When humans began eating flesh and cooking it, and cooking everything else they ate with it, the beneficial bacteria no longer found an environment suitable for growth, in part because cooked foods caused putrefaction in the intestines and in part because evidence suggests that the structure of our intestines changed. Although cooking considerably limits the usable amounts, enough remaining B12 was assimilated to perpetuate the human species.

From survival to revival, the raw vegetarian diet rises above the futility of flesh eating like a phoenix out of the fire. Once your body is cleansed through periodic fasting and continues to be so maintained through proper diet, in which case you need not fast or not so often, the intestines could again provide a home for friendly bacteria. Yet the problem is not just of production, but of absorption. Even carnivores taking pills daily with potencies of 1,000 mcgs can remain deficient.

[Reader advisory: Reading about cancer could cause worry about cancer, and worrying about cancer could cause cancer; so if this advisory worries you, skip this next paragraph.] Meanwhile the rate of carnivores who die from diet-related cancer and heart disease is hundreds if not thousands of times higher compared to vegans who show even slight signs of B12 deficiency. Repeat: carnivores who die compared to vegans who show even slight signs. So why are we even discussing this? Why? Because of carnivore-dominated news media. While one out of four Americans dies of cancer, according to the American Cancer Society one-third of all cancer deaths are related to improper diet. In 1996, its Committee on Diet,

Nutrition and Cancer issued seven simple guidelines to prevent cancer. Here's one of them: "Choose most of the foods you eat from plant sources." Here's another: "Limit your intake of high-fat foods, particularly from animal sources." Like Buddha's supplicant who fruitlessly went in search of mustard seed from a household that had not experienced death, we all have friends and family members who have died of cancer. But I have yet to learn of any contemporary vegan who died from B12 deficiency, and I have yet to meet any vegan who even displayed symptoms of deficiency. Most of the vegans about whom I can speak personally tend to eat a diet more toward raw, and to shun vitamin pills; but maybe, just maybe, they clandestinely swallow down B12 pills with their stiff drinks of carrot juice cocktails.

Herein could be the key that opens the door for raw foods for all, though no one is forced to enter: B12 is found in or on plants, but in amounts so small that cooking destroys all of it, and a toxic body assimilates none of it. The elusive nutrient is rumored to be found in sea vegetables and algae, though some warn that it is an analog form of no use to the human body. And it is rumored to be produced in cultured live raw foods such as nut cheeses, though some warn that in such uncontrolled cultures other harmful bacteria can also grow alongside the beneficial ones. It is also produced by microorganisms found on fruits and vegetables as long as no pesticides or fungicides inhibit their growth. This means adhering as strictly as possible to a diet of organically grown foods. Such foods also may not need rinsing, which is a consideration since all B vitamins are water soluble. Speaking of rinsing, the microorganism is said to be growing among most batches of homegrown sprouts.

All this information was garnered from vegetarian periodicals and books written by zealots occasionally as full of baloney and guilty of fabrications and misrepresentations as any other fanatics intent on changing the world. So don't believe any of the above. Unconvinced? Worry will harm you more than any vitamin deficiency, so go ahead and take a 50 mcg pill once a week. Be assured that the B12 marketed in tablets is of vegan origin. Better still, because the family of B vitamins works synergistically, take a B-complex pill that includes all the other B vitamins, too. Or eat a tablespoon a day of nutritional yeast, the kind labeled with B12 added.

To paraphrase Prince Hamlet: "B12 or not B12, that is the question."

6. Is there an alternative to wheat germ?

Wheat germ is a fractured food, no more wholesome than the white flour from which it was milled. It has all those vitamins, minerals, and protein that the white flour lacks, but unlisted on its label of contents is rancidity, which white flour also lacks. As important as eating foods raw is eating foods whole. Stored at room temperature, wheat kernels will maintain freshness for months, raw wheat germ for but a few days. Raw wheat germ when fresh is golden yellow and tastes sweet, but those stored unrefrigerasted on store shelves are dull brown and taste terrible. Toasted wheat germ does not deteriorate as quickly, but that is because much of its value is initially destroyed in the toasting process. The alternative to wheat germ is simply the whole wheat kernel either sprouted for two days or grown into grass for ten.

Once nature's protective coatings are penetrated, foods must be wrapped in a very large and cumbersome artificial shell, the refrigerator. Unrefined, expeller-pressed oils are also fractured foods prone to rancidity, and so must be chilled; but they are unnecessary in a diet that includes lots of nuts and seeds. One food with as much nutritional punch as wheat germ that needs no refrigeration is brewer's yeast, but it tastes more vile than rancid wheat germ. Anything with such a taste must be of questionable origin, and indeed it is: beer. Primary-grown yeasts, also called nutritional yeasts, which taste much better, also are of a doubtful origin: molasses.

Yet there is neither alcohol in brewer's yeast, nor sugar in those primary-grown. Baker's yeast, used to raise bread, is live so is suitable for a raw food diet; it also tastes better than brewer's yeast, but not by much. It must be eaten only in the morning with nothing other than water, otherwise it will ferment the food mixed with it and cause flatulence. Flatulence may also result from consumption of too much brewer's yeast, but its bad taste serves as a powerful deterrence.

7. Are supplements necessary?

Do not be fooled: no such thing exists as a totally natural vitamin pill. A totally natural vitamin C pill would be the size of an orange, and would contain no more C than does a single orange. Wait a minute, that's no pill; that's an orange. Pills labeled *natural* contain a small amount from natural sources, the rest is mostly synthetic. The family of B vitamins is usually chemicals added to a base of brewer's yeast, and vitamin C (C stands for *Chemical*) to a base of rose hips or acerola. Even when the pill is of a more natural origin, such as oil-based A, D, and E, various chemical processes are employed in extraction, separation, concentration, and preservation.

Anyway, A and D usually come from fish liver oils and are encapsulated in animal gelatin.

The concept of a natural pill is self-contradictory. In what grove does the vitamin C tablet grow? In what field the E capsule stalk? Vitamin E oil is extracted from wheat germ oil via wheat germ via wheat: is that natural? While the eater of sprouted wheat needs no extra E, the typical form of edible wheat is flour, whose milling oxidizes much of the E, and then as bread, whose baking nearly totally destroys it.

If you feel you must resort to supplements, at least make certain they are vegetarian, as they certainly are neither raw nor natural. Most large manufacturers provide a small selection of pills specially marketed to vegetarians. But enough tablet talk. Since the common carnivorism is of muscle and fat rather than organs, the wisely chosen vegetarian diet, raw or cooked, provides more vitamins and minerals per gram of protein than do flesh foods. Disregarding cholesterol, nitrites, and putrefaction, maybe the case is not so much that flesh offers so much less, but that plant food offers so much more. That *more* makes the difference between health and illness, and between life and death.

8. *Any other advice about a raw food diet would be appreciated.*

Nutrition books instruct us in what is good to eat, while cookbooks describe what merely tastes good to eat. Once you begin to eat in order to nourish the body rather than to titillate the tongue, only foods that you know are good *for* you will taste good *to* you. Until then? Follow this simple three-part rule: *Eat foods as Fresh, as Raw, and as Whole as possible.* The phrase *as possible* allows for diversion and diversity.

And the word *Fresh* encompasses also the recent dietary buzz-word *Local*. Should you modify your diet to that suggested here, your presumable improvement in health might be little affected whether you eat 80 percent Fresh, Raw, and Whole, or 99 percent. So here is my food grading system ranging from **A** (for Alive) to **D** (for Dead):

> **A** (all three criteria): *Fresh*, *Raw*, and *Whole*
> **B** (only two criteria): not *Fresh*, or not *Raw*, or not *Whole*
> **C** (solely one criterion): only *Fresh*, or only *Raw*, or only *Whole*
> **D** (no criteria met): not *Fresh*, nor *Raw*, nor *Whole*

For example, UnDead Bread, made of wheat kernels that are sprouted at home and then ground and shaped into wafers just before dinner, is awarded an **A** (*Fresh*, *Raw*, and *Whole*). Essene Bread, made of those same ground wheat sprouts but then baked, rates a **B** (*Fresh* and *Whole*). Whole Wheat Bread, made from commercially milled flour at a faraway bakery, garners only a **C** (only *Whole*). While white flour Blunder Bread flunks out with **D** (not *Fresh* nor *Raw* nor *Whole*), as it's a wonder they can even call it bread.

Organic farming opens a whole new can of earthworms. Naturally, no one wants fungicides or insecticides garnishing their salad greens. But are organically grown foods more natural than those chemically fertilized? Food grown organically does not necessarily mean grown with organic fertilizers. Huh? The USDA-approved organic agriculture industry depends directly upon the flesh industry for its fertilizers of bone meal, blood meal, and animal feces. Yet the farm animals that are the sources of the bone and blood and poop need not themselves be fed or raised organically (nor treated humanely). Factory-farmed chickens, for instance, are intentionally fed insecticides so that their feces will not attract flies; yet that very feces laced with insecticides is used as fertilizer for so-called organically grown produce. Thus the very basis of organic agriculture as currently practiced in the USA is compromised and troubling and far from vegetarian. Hence it is more important that a food be *Fresh*, *Raw*, and *Whole*, that it be **A** or **B**, than that it be OG. Organically groan.

Your last question, unnumbered, is the most important. You ask: *Will you list any qualifications you might have?* My single credential is my health. As I have found what is right for myself, you must find for yourself. Fewer than one or two of every ten Americans looks healthy, and of those who look healthy no one knows how many actually are. I sincerely hope the others are not as unhealthy as they appear. But health is not an end in itself but a means to an end. And it is a means to postpone the final end.

Herbivorously,
Mark

4.

TRAVELING FAST

What, then, do I wish to say? That in order to be moral, people must cease to eat meat? Not at all. I only wish to say that for a good life a certain order of good deeds is indispensable; that if a man's aspirations toward right living be serious, it will inevitably follow one definite sequence; and that in this sequence the first virtue a man will strive after will be temperance, self-renunciation. And in seeking to be temperate a man will inevitably follow one definite sequence, and in this sequence the first thing will be temperance in food, fasting. And in fasting, if he be really and seriously seeking to live a good life, the first thing from which he will abstain will always be the use of animal food, because, to say nothing of the excitation of the passions caused by such food, its use is simply immoral, as it involves the performance of an act which is contrary to the moral feeling—killing.

LEO TOLSTOY
"The First Step"

FIRE!

NOT ENOUGH TIME FOR BOTH, you must rescue either your sibling or your spouse. Who would you choose? (What you really should have chosen is between a brick house and a home of wood.) Suppose the choice is between your mate or your life; you are less indecisive. And suppose between your spouse and a lamb, or between his or her leg and a leg of lamb; the answers are clearer here. Now consider your life or a hundred lives of lambs; here we approach closer to our subject. Vegetarianism, however, is not deciding between your life and an animal; but whether to shorten and torture the lives of about fifteen cattle, ten sheep, twenty-five hogs, one thousand birds, and one thousand fish: these are the rounded-off numbers of rounded-up animals an ill-rounded American inattentively devours in an average life span, and we won't add up the cows milked dry and the chickens who only count their eggs but never hatch them.

Self-defensive carnivores posit this notion: after starving for nearly a month, would you eat a rabbit? This dilemma passes from hypothesis to artifice for two reasons. The first is that such carnivores more than likely are urbanites: the natural world they see is seldom more than feral cats and rats and mice and lice; in resorting to rabbits for their hypothetical food, they forget about the food that nourished the rabbit; they would eat anything that moved, and maybe only things that moved. Yet just as more kinds of vegetables than cuts of meat can be bought at a supermarket, more edible plants than elusive animals can be sought in the wilderness.

The second reason ignores the premises of the first altogether, because the person before starvation and the one during are not the same: vegetarians do resort to carnivorism just as in the same situations carnivores turn into cannibals. The question is how often these situations occur, and the answer is, hardly often enough to be worth consideration. Only when we walk into the movie theater do we enter such Dark Ages: in *The Gold Rush*, when the starved Mack Swain hallucinated Charlie Chaplin into a chicken, that was no joke.

The state of starvation varies from person to person. Ponder two people stranded on a barren island. One might begin a fast at the same time that the other would begin going hungry; so the first likely would live for two months, while the second would perish after barely one. As undeniable as it is unendurable, though the two match in actions and motions, they diverge in reactions and emotions. All matters differ to different minds, and many diseases are only in the mind. Most suffering is an affliction not by a virus but by something just as elusive, a desire. In this instance the desire for food proves fatal before the lack of food. The starved hunter, gun in hand, wants to eat, but is unable; one the faster is able, but wants not. The former for no reason is forced; the other is voluntary and for a real reason.

But more important than mere reasons are causes. A person fasting as a protest or for a cause can endure far more than someone fasting for health. The person living for a cause and an ideal, indeed an ideal cause, lives forever; ideals and the ideas of those ideals are eternal. We are born to give birth to children or to give birth to brain children or to both; if to brain children, then our or others' children will keep them alive after we die. The one ideal cause is not yet known, but a very good cause among a thousand very good causes is vegetarianism. Thus, provided only rabbits as food, a vegetarian might fast for a very good cause.

The uninitiated assume that fasting, if it is good at all, is good only for the cause; fasters know better, they know it is equally good for their health. An Indian fasted to protest British occupation of India, an American to protest American intervention in Vietnam, and both fasted to dislodge wasteful matters from their bodies and troubling matters from their minds. Both armies seemed overwhelming, but not much had to be expelled from the fasters' bodies nor much unburdened from their minds: Gandhi was and Dick Gregory is vegetarian.

Here we will see how vegetarianism and fasting are a pair together, and how the person who is serious about one should consider the other. For fasting stands to gluttony as vegetarianism stands to carnivorism. Some fast to contest an otherwise incurable disease. Others fast to protest an injustice across the seas. For these, so long as they are attentive to a few rules, the consequence is not just in heaven but in health.

But let us be realistic. Few causes demand the devotion of an entire life, few forests are large enough that we might be lost in their midst for weeks, and few fires rage where we are forced to choose between our sibling and our spouse. This third most archetypal dilemma involving the right to leave someone to the flames is the most absurd and least likely to occur. It is one thing to leave someone to the flames, another to throw someone onto the flames: but this is just what is commonly done to animals. Forgetting forests and fires, we had better remember factory farms.

It is improbable that we will ever have to search for food on hands and knees and grovel in the gravel, or be forced to sleep in fields and trees when we travel; we will travel by train or plane and sleep in motels or hotels. So we will have to search, not for meat, but only for some fresh fruit or whole grain bread. On a short trip we might pack our own food, but on longer excursions a wee bit of white sugar here, a morsel of white bread there, a few drips of white milk, and even a few dabs of white lard all somehow manage to intrude their way onto our plates and before our paths.

The detour is greatest if on a longer tour, say of Europe. On such journeys the strength of our convictions truly are tested. In Southern Italy, for example, whole wheat pasta is fed only to the sick and dying, the only ones willing to squander an extra euro for a minute more, though, to be fair, in all of Italy a third of the bread is whole grain and salt-free. A hundred years ago only the rich could afford white food; now that the cycle has come half circle, we might instead cross the Alps to Switzerland, where whole-kernel bread outsells white, where the healthy are very healthy, and where the rich are very rich. Typically, in Zurich we find Europe's largest and most luxurious vegetarian restaurant, and also its most expensive. Though health is our greatest wealth, should the wealthy be the only ones healthy?

Instead of eating out, we can either not go out or not eat. The first alternative is a restriction on our lives, but the second is a great freedom. Vegetarian restaurants are not found everywhere, especially once we leave our American coasts. The United States consists of three demographic regions: there is the East Coast, and the West Coast, and everything in between is The South. Eventually we would eat out of the ordinary sordid greasy spoon. The vegetarian sections on the menus of Chinese-American or Thai-American restaurants are seldom the safe havens that vegetarians delude themselves into believing they have found. Both cultural and language barriers make it difficult to communicate to waiters that garlic sauces made with fish or oysters or crabs disqualify the dish as vegetarian. Patronizing is compromising, so travelers should fast simply to protest silently the large numbers of charcoal-broil charnel houses. That the protest is silent is no coincidence. The "word fast" is analogous to the food fast: indeed some close their mouths to speech at the same time as to sustenance. Pythagoras required his disciples to fast forty days before admitting them under his tutelage. This was before they could hear anything, much less say anything. Christ fasted forty days before he began to preach. Anaxarchus, the Greek philosopher, was tortured by Nicocreon, the King of Cyprus, to betray the names of fellow conspirators, but instead of talking bit out his tongue and spat it in the tyrant's face. He did this after having been deprived of food for many days. Monks' fasts are as well known as their taciturnity: Trappists are silent; Buddhists, Jains, Benedictines, Carthusians, and Trappists are vegetarians; just about all of them fast; and the majority who speak, speak softly.

This is all serious, yet may seem somewhat mysterious to the person who has never fasted. When fasting, normally obscure and unnoticed stimuli are magnified into either very repulsive or very attractive sights, sounds, smells, and tactile sensations, once the all-too-overwhelming taste buds have been set to rest. The blind person, and to a lesser and more momentary degree the blindfolded person, develops keener hearing to compensate for lost sight. Likewise, after a fast, food tastes better than ever before. Even during the fast, mountain spring water could prove to be the most delicious of all meals. In contrast, bad smells could become so offensive that we would break the fast to be no longer vulnerable to them, particularly to flesh oxidizing in an oven. But the most disturbing of all obstructions is noise so loud that even our shouts for silence go unheard. Here speech fasting is necessary. We shut up. We want to say "Shut Up!" Instead, we set the example; simply and purely and silently, we ourselves shut up.

An entire day could be spent traveling through the cornfields of Illinois without once seeing any cattle for whose mouths the corn is grown. Another entire day could be devoted to roaming through the cattle country of Texas without once seeing any humans for whose mouths the cattle are raised. That is all a great waste of space, where trees once grew in Illinois or could someday be cultivated in Texas. But then, the trees would probably be milled into paper, most of which is also a great waste of space. Few new books are good because most good books are no longer new. The same is true for books on food, and for food itself: even flesh foods are older than cakes, chips, pies, and fries. We do better reading good books than none, but also no books than bad. The same is truer for books on food and truest for food itself: better to eat nothing that is food than food that is nothing.

Reading in itself accomplishes little. Some read aloud to themselves to avoid having to think for themselves, yet they let the author's thoughts pass through them unassimilated. Wearing blinders to the passing landscapes, readers can be like sleepy drivers attentive only to reaching their distant destinations. Or some choose authors precisely because of the book's poverty of thought. Readers can be compared to eaters, bestseller lists to quick, but hardly quickening, foods. Full digestion of the food's total nutrition slips by when people barely chew, and they seldom give their stomachs a rest before stuffing them anew. This is said with the hope that nourishment actually resides in the food; yet just as people may employ language not to express thoughts but to conceal that they have none, the boxes and cans on supermarket shelves are adorned with bright colors and beguiling names to deter from the fact that the packages lack real contents. Consequently, people develop all sorts of digestive deficiency diseases, such as colitis and diverticulitis. A bland diet of the very foods that caused the illnesses is prescribed by their doctors, the bland leading the bland. Had the patients fasted instead, they would be giving long needed rests to both their stomachs and their doctors.

Where nothing is put in, nothing can be gotten out. No deposit, no return. Exhaling is possibly more important than inhaling, and at times fasting is more important than eating. Such times certainly include when we are away from home. No greater effort is needed to eat a vegetable food than a flesh food, a nourishing food than a junk food, so long as we are at home. Elsewhere, excuses substitute for choices. Though we may fast on the road, eventually when we return to home sweet home we will have to return to food, and for breaking a fast, preferably fruits. The human body is too imperfect to live its whole life fasting. We have no need for pretenses: we are only human. Regarding our humanity, sages throughout the ages have said that the answers to our questions will come, if they come at all, through contemplation and fasting. And most questions amount to one: What are we?

If we are what we eat, then we must ask: What to eat? And from where does what we eat come? Our food either comes directly from plants, or from animals who come from plants. In either case, we indirectly come from what plants come from, which is the sun, so we are really eating the sun as our main course, with a little earth, moon, and stars as side dishes. Most of all, plants depend upon the sun, and therefore so do we. If only we could come directly from and depend solely upon the sun! Though green with envy, we are not green with chlorophyll. As far as we can see, the sun is the one source to which we owe existence. The ancients, who worshipped the sun, knew from where they had come; but we seem to have forgotten. We see only that we have come from the ancients, so we deify them instead: for instance, Abraham, Moses,

Jesus, Zoroaster, Krishna, Buddha, and Muhammad, to name just a few. And whereas the ancients believed the first persons born were the stars and the planets, we refer to them under the pseudonyms Adam and Eve.

If our bodies are our temples, some people worship their temples rather than the gods thought to dwell within them. Similarly, contemporary "sun worshippers" confuse symbol for sacrament, and they actually worship their bodies, not the sun. They can be discerned by a darker tone of skin color, and sometimes by a deeper degree of skin cancer. Despite their confusion, the sun shines its blessings upon them, day after long hot summer day. The sun's energy may even enable them to eat slightly less at meals, because the usual transfers of sun energy to plant foods to human energy dispenses with the intermediary plant, and instead they gain some nourishment straight from the sun. It must be emphasized that this direct energy transfer from sun to human, if it exists at all, is barely perceptible; worshippers could sit all day beneath the sun and need only one less mouthful of food. That is how inefficient we animals all are at harnessing solar energy. At the same time, we are at constant risk of exposing ourselves to solar energy overload, which we manifest as sunstroke. Thus we need sun-nourished plants not merely for food but also for shade. Shade is one thing, but darkness quite another. Plants, angling their leaves toward the sun, feed upon the light; but animals who feed upon light-infused plants are shade and shadows; and animals who feed on shadowy animals are darkness. Try as we may to seek the light, one place we are not likely to find it is an eviscerated corpse drained of life.

Like the tax collector who expends ninety-nine cents to expunge a dollar, the carnivore indulges in a waste of energy by routing light through four transformers: one, sun energy to plant matter; two, plant matter to animal matter; three, animal matter to human matter; four, human matter to human energy. The pervasive unwillingness to gather one's plants for oneself, but instead to depend upon a cow or a pig or a chicken to do it, is due to society's aggregate equivalent of individual laziness. Growing plants in our gardens, gathering them in our hands, creating meals from them in our kitchens, are all concerns for us who wish to do as many chores for ourselves as possible. We can excuse ourselves for our dependence upon plants, and maybe for our dependence upon farmers; but why try to justify any additional dependence upon a cow or a pig or a chicken?

Rudolf Steiner, in *Problems of Nutrition*, posits that when eating plants, humans are compelled to do a lot of internal work themselves because plants do not manufacture animal fat. The vegetarian human body thus must produce fat of its own, an activity otherwise spared when consuming the ready-made fat of flesh food. He believed vegetarians are lords and creators of their bodies; but carnivores, by shunning the task of fat formation and passing it on to the animals they eat, remain mere spectators and thus forestall their own spiritual growth. We might deduce from this that the whole phenomenon of spirituality boils down to the question of energy, that spirit is the essence of energy that animates, and that the greater we are spiritually developed the more we are self-animated. It is no coincidence that the Christian day of worship falls on the day named for the sun.

Whether it is the light or the warmth from the sun that is most needed is unclear. A tomato plant depends upon sunlight for growth, but a tomato can ripen in a dark room when warm. This much is certain: the tropical regions on the earth's surface are warmest because they receive the most direct light. Of all plants, trees with their thousands of leaves gather the most light; of all fruits from trees, tropical fruits from latitudes of fewest degrees are the "lightest." Excluding severe hypoglycemics among us, our diets benefit from a proportionate increase in fruits, and particularly in tropical or semi-tropical fruits. Of all fruits the mango is just about the sweetest, the papaya the most soothing, and the avocado the most nutritious. Eskimos, to whom fruits from trees are hardly forbidden but simply unavailable, are known for their diminished longevity. This could be as much due to the flesh they eat as to the fruits they lack.

Of everything we eat, fruits contain the greatest concentration of sun energy. We in turn need the least exertion of our own energy to transform that plant matter into human matter: fruits generally require an hour to be digested, fruit juices half an hour, as opposed to four hours for flesh. In all fairness, we must admit that unsoaked nuts take four hours, too; yet soaked nuts, requiring less than two hours, become more like fruits. And the opposite is true: dried fruits are more like nuts and need two hours. So, we soak nuts and dried fruits before eating them.

The foods to eat just before and just after a fast are fruits. This parodies the classical form of the sonata, as in a Beethoven string quartet: ACA. Fruits are the foods most similar to juice just as fruit juices are the liquids most similar to water. Far more gradual, and therefore more effective transitions occur when adjoining the days of fasting by days of drinking fruit juices, and days of fruit juices by days of eating fruits. Here we hear, if we have the ear, the *andante* movement in Op. 132 which Beethoven offered as a prayer of holy thanksgiving for recovery from a nearly fatal illness: ABCBA. Clearly, fasting is best accompanied in priority and posteriority by eating lightly.

Lifelong fasters who have practiced various techniques and studied the experiences of their peers and their forebears nearly unanimously agree that the best whole food upon which to break a fast is fruit, while absolutely no one recommends flesh. Eating flesh, or pizza, or cake, or fries is bad enough, but it is worse to eat them as the last meal preceding or the first following a fast. Alternatively, fasting can be undertaken precisely because such a meal has been eaten; this strategy ignores all else and employs the fast as a defense solely for its cleansing effects. But fruits best break fasts: those that flush through the body with the greatest of ease are melons, plums, grapes, and the blackest cherries. Flesh, however, will clog the flow like a plug, causing the stagnant waters to become polluted. Frankfurters are made of and some cold cuts are even encased in cow intestinal walls, so no wonder they clog our own intestines.

Fasting metaphorically turns the human body upside down and inside out; what go inside out are the toxins, and upside down are the intestines. Though nothing is eaten, much waste is eliminated. The stupor of the first fasts is burdensome, but compensated by the vigor of the first days after them. Even those who maintain a healthful diet walk around with five pounds of crap in their intestines; a first fast will be the most effective means of dislodging it, and fairly regular fasts thereafter will keep out the crap.

Although digesting fruit is less an effort than digesting flesh, digesting nothing is the least of all efforts. Not doing something is easy; it may be difficult to begin again to do the thing left long undone. Fasting is easy, breaking the fast hard. The first fast, however, is the most troublesome and uncomfortable because of what comes out, while the first day of eating after any fast can be catastrophic precisely because of what does not come out. Little effort is necessary to eat nothing, but after breaking the fast more effort is needed to eat a little than to eat a lot. The worst thing we can do is gorge ourselves, like a liberated Tantalus maddened by hunger.

A modified form of fasting is a lengthy diet of just fruit juices. Some eat whole fruits and consider that a kind of fast, too. The implication should be obvious. Every argument favoring carnivorism can be inferred to periodic cannibalism, particularly cannibalism upon enemies in times of war, in the same manner that any argument favoring vegetarianism can be inferred to periodic fasting. Likewise, factors that favor fasting extend to vegetarianism. Vegetarians whose diet includes large proportions of fruit need hardly fast and need hardly be concerned about the task of breaking it when they do. Fewer toxins are excreted because fewer are ingested. The opposite of fruit is flesh: Arnold Ehret warns carnivores to fast with great caution since humans' own toxins are already too much; the stampede of the animals' as well could do a lot of harm before doing any good.

Ehret may not have been the record-breaker of last century's fasters but he is probably the most well known. He also knew very well what he was doing. What must be emphasized is that he knew what he was doing for himself, and for himself alone. As with eating, proper ways of abstention from eating must be found out for ourselves. Who would not rather experience life for oneself than read the conjectures of a hundred philosophers and the exegeses of a hundred thousand professors of philosophy? Most important, after learning about fasting for ourselves, we will learn a lot about ourselves. When we eat, the body directs energy to digestion, to overcome food to make it become ourselves. But when we fast, energy can instead be directed simply to becoming ourselves. We look into the mirror and do not recognize our faces; we speak and do not recognize our voices; we think and do not recognize our thoughts. We become persons other than normally known, persons otherwise hidden deep within. But we are not transformed, nor are our old selves forgotten; rather, our conception of our old selves is forgotten; we suddenly see and hear as though for the first time.

Now our question must be, "How to fast?" Techniques vary. For some, eating only apples is a form of fasting, while for others it is drinking only apple juice. Some say it is imperative to drink some kind of fresh fruit juice, others to drink herb teas with lemon. Some define fasting as drinking only water and specify spring water because the distilled kind drains the body of minerals. Others say to drink distilled water precisely because those minerals are inorganic deposits for which the body has no use. Some recommend continuing the fast until the mucus coating on the tongue clears, others until hunger reappears. Some assert the necessity of enemas, others warn against them except in the most extreme emergencies.

It is easy to see that the science of abstention from nourishment is as confusing as that of procuring it. We can ignore the whole matter and choose never to fast, though this is comparable to developing an aversion to drinking water because of never having learned to swim. This much we know: we are as wise to ignore those books that advise how not to eat but not how to eat. In the late 1970s, many fasting books with calligraphic titles and psychedelic covers appeared whose single synonym for the subject was "weight loss." These books, written by and for average carnivores, appeared as quickly as a fad and disappeared as quickly as a fashion. We whose concerns are nutritional and not cosmetic must be vigilant to discern the quick from the dead. Like figs and dates, which are as appetizing dried as fresh, the serious books on fasting have remained in print for years; and the best are an essential part of a larger system of diet and living. Their emphasis is on fasting as part of a sane system of eating; they speak equally of sustenance, not just abstinence. Among the aforementioned authors in chapter 2, those that discuss fasting in depth are Bragg, Shelton, Ehret, Kulvinskas, Clement, and Cousens. Fasting books, good or bad, need not be read for us to discover their differences. A glance is enough: we can tell a health book by its back cover. The meritorious, serious fasting books display photographs of their authors (unless they wish to perpetuate their obscurity), whose pictures of health promote their contents. The meretricious, fake fasting books dare not exhibit their authors, who often have too much to hide. Of fad books that did picture the author, the most notorious was a liquid animal protein advocate, shown aiming a fat finger at an unseen target, like Moses pointing to the promised land into which he is forbidden entry.

It hardly occurs to the polluted and deluded to fast. This is perhaps to be expected. If many had this notion, no delusion would exist: what the deluded most need is what they least perceive or believe. Meanwhile they settle for pills and potions, symbols of and substitutes for what they seek, and as many die from their pills as from their ills. All fasting does is assure the body a chance to cure itself; yet after a fast, already healthy people will feel even healthier, and those who eat judiciously and fast regularly can feel fine when eating, but even better when not. Huh? The Greek gods dined on ambrosia and nectar, but our every mouthful reminds us of our mortality. For the cast-iron pot, we give up an iron stomach, and end up with a pot belly. Humanity, bulbous-bellied but still its eyes bigger than its mouth, will never return to peace with its gods by saying grace at any dinner table. Fruit alone will not provide solace; the apple was the provocation in the first place.

The fasts of Western religions last only one day as in Judaism, or only during the day as in Islam, or only from one food as in Christianity. Fasting for only a day is just long enough to begin to feel hunger, but not long enough for its gnawing to subside, as will happen by the second or third day. Even when not fasting, healthful eaters and frequent fasters rarely experience hunger; hunger is an ill omen, a nudge in the ribs to remind sufferers of lives gone wrong. A forgotten meal or first fasting day may cause only a funny feeling in the throat. But try telling this to someone on the first day of the first fast! Initiates will need more than just assurances; they will need faith. As for seeing gods, instead they will see only a lot of mucus, feces, and maybe even vomit. Determination to persist beyond the first day of hunger, the second day possibly of dizziness, and perhaps a third day of nausea, is of no consequence if we are unprepared for the final day of reckoning, the day we break the fast. Wrongly turning to inappropriate foods assures that nothing is gained, and something even lost.

Along with the leap of faith is needed the sweep of faith: the sweep of the intestines, not just the intentions. The leap loosens the mental straitjacket that even the most rational wear, while the sweep loosens the bowels. Following the leaping and sweeping comes the reaping: after the intestines are cleared of crap, we who maintain a wholly whole and mostly raw

diet will no longer need nutrients in the gross amounts speci-
fied for others. Unlike our own, the heavy-meat and sugar-
sweet diet of complicated cookery (which cooks everything)
and complex food combinations (which combines everything)
requires gross quantities of nutrients merely to cut through a
nearly impenetrable digestive system, stuck with muck.

The case of B12 illustrates this point precisely. Dietary dos-
age recommendations apply to the typical consumer of lots of
fat and protein from lots of flesh and milk, as well as lots of fluff
from lots of white food. But humans who fast, drink no alcohol, smoke no tobacco, and eat mostly whole raw plant foods
will need far less of the vitamin than cooked-food carnivores
need. Flesh and milk, the most often cited sources of the vitamin, contain also the most saturated fats; deficiencies develop
in laboratory animals fed adequate amounts of B12, but also
high amounts of fat. Grease clogs drains. Similarly, diets high
in animal protein deplete the vitamin, and diets dominated
by white foods double the B12 required by baboons. These
are insights already adduced by vegetarians, but only the sufferings of lab animals knocks this into the skulls of scientists.

Until we fast, all reasoning concerning it supports opin-
ion but does not prove it; its merits will remain too fantastic
to believe or too confusing to understand. But once we have
put the horse of experience in front of the cart of rationality, excessive needs for nutrients are not the only extraneous
things eliminated. The desire for food disappears after the
first day of a fast, and other desires lose hold on later days. For
instance, after about three days we might walk past the store
window that displays that new coat eyed so enviously previously, but today winter will seem very far away and we will
remember our other three coats, two more than needed. By

the fifth day, all sexual impulses for moonlight liaisons eclipse into moonlight sonatas. Gandhi rarely discussed fasting without mentioning celibacy. Wooing and eating and drinking are pleasures undeniably, but not undeniable; be they as they may, they are pleasures only of the body. Denying sex and food and drink are also pleasures, but of the soul.

Desires are cast behind not just during fasts but, if fasts are regularly conducted, between them as well. If one has not yet done so, vegetarianism will surely be embraced. While Moses fasted for forty days and forty nights the first time atop Mount Sinai, his people reverted to worshipping a calf that, lucky for the calf, was made of gold instead of flesh and blood. Seeing this, Moses realized his generation was not ready for a new life. So he fasted for another forty days and forty nights, awaiting new instructions. Then he led them on a pilgrimage in the desert for forty years until new generations grew new bodies; only then were they prepared for their new lives. The wandering was a sort of fast in preparation for entrance into a new land.

The carnivore converting to vegetarianism, the vegetarian to veganism, the vegan to raw foods, all more assuredly would surmount the obstacles along life's way if they fasted during their transitions into new lives. Their fasts would detoxify their bodies during the course of a few days, rather than their new diets doing so during several months, and few would misattribute to their new vegetarian diet the sickness that comes from cleansing. The neophyte's nausea does not come directly from vegetarianism or from fasting. Rather, nausea comes from cleansing; it is the cleansing that comes directly from vegetarianism or from fasting. Those who complain of tiredness and headaches during their first month of vegetarianism blame their ills on doing without flesh food rather than on having done with it for so long. Quick to behead the messenger who brings bad news, they revert to carnivorism and thereby continue chopping off a lot of other heads.

If we ignore all bad news, it will cease to be given to us. Sycophants to sickness are impatient: willing to try everything once, they rarely try anything twice. Packing up to move to a new home is easy if we never got around to unpacking in our old one, but better still is dumping the wasteful baggage rather than dragging it along. Old habits are as much embedded in our minds as is old feces impacted in our intestines. Too many people accept both as normal modes of life. But such a life is that of the elderly man who carried a chair wherever he went so that whenever he tired he had something close at hand upon which to sit and rest. He felt grateful for the chair, yet never realized that what made him so exhausted was his transporting it.

Fully a year may be necessary for initiates to reap any new regimen's results, so its adaptation must be based largely on faith. Fasting enhances graceful and durable transitions, both physically and spiritually, in regards to both abstinence and sustenance. Gandhi developed spiritually so intensely in his later life that he fasted as many days as he ate; when he did eat he limited his menu to five items a day, and he ate only between sunrise and sunset. His mind was elsewhere than on just food, or perhaps it was on both everything under the sun, and everything above it.

A stage could eventually be reached when fasting is no longer necessary. Toxins, a normal product of metabolism, should be no greater than the healthy body is capable of expelling. A few years of periodic fasting should rid the body of the old toxic load, and regular adherence to a raw vegetarian diet should prevent or at least reduce any new one. A sign that the body is renewed is unanticipated difficulty in fasting. The negative proof of this are the infirm who lose appetite during their illness, whose burdened bodies attempt to fast, but whose entrenched minds are unwilling. Those who willfully and easily fast probably need to do so until it no longer is so needed. So an umbilical tie is severed, and the fast becomes a part of the past.

We all need green. It is a metaphysical if not physical fact that no color renders rest so efficiently and deeply to its viewer. Chlorophyll is green, thus leaves are green, thus trees mostly are green, thus forests mostly are green. Where climates are coldest, where winters are whitest, leaves remain green year round. Suburbanites grow gardens as hobbies, and even city dwellers cultivate house plants by their soot-stained windows to compensate for what they do not see outside. But a woodsman, whose cabin is made of the very trees surrounding his home, needs no windows.

One reason the American urban populace is so frenetic is that its diet of fried foods, white foods, and flesh foods is particularly high in phosphorus, which disturbs the balance of calcium and magnesium, which causes nervous behavior: mineral imbalance is but a step toward mental imbalance. Another instigating factor is that urbanites rarely see green, so "lose their cool" and "see red," which opposes green on the color wheel. And what is chlorophyll? The substance found outside the body that is most nearly identical to the hemoglobin inside. They differ molecularly only where hemoglobin contains iron, chlorophyll contains magnesium; chromatically, blood is red, while leaves are green. Complementary colors create harmony in our homes; likewise in our more inner interiors. Those who see green least have a greater need for eating it. Of any vegetables that urbanites might hope to grow, their freshest greens are their sprouts and seedlings of indoor windowsill and kitchen cabinet gardens.

With fewer opportunities to see green, city folks should eat less flesh: their own bodies are red enough. The more red flesh eaten, the more are green vegetables needed to match. Hence bottomless salad bowls frequently accompany mistaken main courses at steak houses. Farmers who not only grow their own green but kill their own red can better get by eating flesh than can urbanites. Just as Old Masters mixed their own paints from pigments often from the very land they lived on, called earth colors, carnivores who endeavor to view a clear picture of reality should spill the blood of the animals they live on. Those who ignore mineral balances, color harmonies, and moral imperatives should forewarn others. In the spirit of the Friends of Animals bumper sticker *Warning: I Break for Animals*, they should affix on their cars the bumper sticker *Warning: I Breakfast on Animals*, so that others might know to steer clear of their peers reared on steer.

Chlorophyll benefits everyone, not just the carnivore. Some get by though eating few greens by eating no reds. Fruits comprise all the colors in between, and again take position alongside sprouts as the opposite of flesh: a fruit generally ripens from green to red, while flesh putrefies from red to green. Among the few green "fruit-fruits" is the avocado, the platypus of plants, nutritionally more like a vegetable and digestibly more like a nut. Another green fruit is the lime, which goes very well with the avocado. Food-combination and protein-complement charts could probably be drawn according to color alone. In fact, a whole healing discipline uses color as its basic criterion for what to eat. But older than chromo-therapy is healing by fasting, whose diet consumes no color: clear water and clean air both are colorless. In the pursuit of clean air, those who fast in cities should do so on weekends when factories are less active and car traffic less congested. And though they might resort to faucet water at other times, they should drink spring or distilled water. Clear fruit juices and herb teas might be indulged by the faster, since these are translucent rather than opaque.

The interaction of colors relates to fasting in still stranger ways. When a painter mixes all the colors on the palette, no matter how intense the yellow or deep the blue or bright the red, it all comes out dull brown. The same for eating, for mixing all the colors under the palate: no matter how green the spinach or red the raspberry or yellow the lemon or orange the orange or even white the flour and the sugar, it, too, all comes out a dull brown. Were the fasting process merely material, nothing would come out where nothing was put in; quite the contrary, color has as much to do with not eating as with eating. Bowels still will move, but instead of the brown color from mixing everything, in the absence of food the bowels show the absence of color: black. Black is associated with the opposite of white, white being the color of light, and light being the essence of life. This is a great reason for fasting only once if we never fast again, for it is on the first fast that we get out the most black. We have already observed that in conjunction with a raw veg-etarian diet, fasting can become superfluous. The rare people who subsist solely on fruits never need fast since their diet is full of life and light, not death and darkness.

Lumberjacks catch neither Chestnut nor Dutch Elm Disease, and farmers are immune to the blights to which their crops succumb. But many illnesses in the chicken coop are contagious to their keepers; a tubercular cow transmits her bacteria through raw milk; and trichinosis is communicable to anyone who brings home the bacon. The lower along the twisted chain of life from which we eat, the less incidence of disease we receive from our food. Fasting extends these ends so far down the line that we bend below it, escape it, and transcend it. We have already observed that the scale of eaten animal life to eater human life registers as one day more of animal eating equaling one day less of human living. Such a system of subtraction carries no place for addition; that is the measure where fasting makes its mark. Every day fasted is an extra day of life, because as far as the body's metabolism is concerned, a day of rest from the toils of digestion is a day not lived. Thus the person who fasts a day a week for an entire lifetime may live eighty years, not just seventy. Proof of this need not be sought in any library stack, livery stable, or operating table. All we need to do is listen to the beats of our own hearts: pulse rates lower with each day of fasting, same as with animals in hibernation. Clues become keys, keys become knowledge, so long as we have found the door of disquisition. The pulse is the clue, the body is the key, health is the door, and through long life comes knowledge. We all are born with the keys to happiness, but are left to our own devices in finding our doors.

The Bible warns that he who does not fast cannot enter the kingdom of heaven. It may be safer to say that one way among many ways of achieving eternal life is through fasting. But it has been "only" long life, not eternal life, about which we here have spoken, and then only in token. Eve's temptation of the apple is a parable of gluttony, a sin from which other little sins and other little Adams and little Eves sprout and stem. Noah should have fasted for those forty days and forty nights while tossing upon the sea of wrath, but instead turned the ark into a cupboard and brought food along for everybody. This must have meant greens for lambs, lambs for lions, and greens and lambs for Noah. Though not attributing it to his dereliction of duty, only beginning with Noah does the Bible mention human carnivorism. To Adam was given "every plant yielding seed" and "every tree with seed in its fruit"; but Noah got "every moving thing that lives." From Noah onward, the stench of burning flesh became a "pleasing odor" to the Lord, and animals fell into categories of those to be sacrificed and those not, those to be eaten and those not, and the four more permutations of their combinations. And before Noah, people lived to 700 and 900 years old, Methuselah to 969; but after Noah, they lived only to 120 and 150. Whether an ancient year was shorter than our own is not what we most immediately might question; what we must wonder is whether a life of flesh eating is shorter than of fruit eating.

All things considered, a remaining question is: "Why does not everyone fast?" And a correlate: "Why is not everyone a vegetarian?" We will unfortunately disregard the first, leave until later the second, and have to be content with addressing a third question: "Why does not every vegetarian fast?" An objection has sometimes been raised by vegetarians that fasting is an extreme form of carnivorism, a self-cannibalism. Strange that vegetarians cast doubt on such a useful tool and its many toolmakers; instead they should defame Frank Perdue, Oscar Mayer, and Colonel Sanders.

Once upon a time, a city supermarket Daniel Boone intended to kill a tender chicken but slipped and, instead of its head, he chopped off his own hand. Since he was as hungry for something on his plate as the chicken was hasty to make its escape, he quickly figured that if he could eat pig's knuckles he might as well eat his own knuckles. Instead of a ham sandwich he prepared a hand sandwich, like Harpo Marx spreading mustard not on the hot dog but on the hot dog vendor, biting into his hand between two slices of bread. The next day, recalling his mother's recipe for fried chicken handed down from generation to generation in his old Kentucky home, he dipped the leftover in batter, rolled the hand in bread crumbs, shook the hand, and then fried it in chicken fat. "They snatch on the right, but are still hungry; and they devour on the left, but are not satisfied; each devours the flesh of his arm…and his hand is stretched out still" (Isaiah 9:20–21).

Chicken-Fried Kentuckian.

5.

THE MILKY WAY

Those who lament over the barbarism that comes out of
barbarism are like people who wish to eat their veal with-
out slaughtering the calf. They are willing to eat the calf,
but they dislike the sight of blood. They are easily satisfied
if the butcher washes his hands before weighing the meat.

BERTOLT BRECHT
"Writing the Truth: Five Difficulties"

WRITING EXISTS AT ONCE *for* those who read, and *against* those who do not read. If you have read thus far, the preceding was probably for you; but if you believe you drink your milk "without slaughtering the calf," the following shall be against you. However, mere writing and reading neither postulate nor prove a thing. We must remember that what we read concerning what to eat is written by those who might not hesitate to lie through their keyboard if either themselves or their merchants stand to gain a profit from it. And even where something relatively truthful is told, it is often by those neither old enough nor bold enough to put it into practice.

The West at once possesses the tallest and most durable houses of worship, yet the greatest and most destructive warships and the largest and most efficient slaughterhouses. Bad enough to kill; worse to harm and then kill; worst to harm, to continue harming, and yet not kill. Some suffering can be so great that killing is almost kind: putting the soul out of its body also means putting the body out of its pain. *Killing* implies immediacy; *harming* denotes slow prolonged death. Still, *humane slaughter*, a gross contradiction of adjective with noun, can be expedient if every possible effort first to end the suffering has failed. Factory-farming conditions by which most milk and eggs are produced cause great suffering to cows, to their calves, and to chickens. Domastication [sic] of animals compares to slavery of humans, and in place of the few surviving species of animal predators has evolved a whole new race of human creditors, milking them dry.

Vegetarians who drink milk and eat cheese and eggs have three choices of change: killing animals, thus ending their suffering, and eating the flesh, thus wasting no food (thereby ceasing to be vegetarians); or keeping goats in sheds and chickens in kitchens, thus assuring their well-being, and eating only their milk and eggs (thereby remaining lacto-ovo-vegetarians); or renouncing milk and eggs altogether (thereby becoming vegans). Much is heralded about national identity and *ethnic* cuisine; let us unite to form a new vegan nation with an *ethic* cuisine.

Abandoning these animal products also means abandoning their animal producers, but since everyone is not becoming a vegetarian, nor would do so overnight, no one need wait up late at night worrying until the cows come home. Meantime, we should worry that the cows *are* home. The inhumane exploitation of cow and chicken has already been eloquently exposed by Peter Singer in *Animal Liberation*, and thirty years later revisited in his book co-authored with animal rights attorney Jim Mason, *The Way We Eat*. So here we shall forego enlisting in the chorus of complaint. But of the cow's calves and the chicken's chicks, something need be said.

The egg industry calls egg-laying hens *layers*, as opposed to hens and roosters that the flesh industry calls *broilers*. Such egg-laying hens have no husbands to peck, and all their lives count their chickens before they hatch. As long as two-day-old chicks are not considered delicacies from which famous French chefs can carve out their culinary crimes, the chicks do not join the ranks of other animal children such as lambs and calves who pass through the gates of the teeth of time and disappear down the esophagi of eternity. Thus the lack of chicks is one aspect in favor of the egg industry over the milk. Farmers and those they feed argue that factory farming at least brings animals into this world that might otherwise never be snatched from the other. They retort that selfhood is not justifiable at the cost of slavery and suffering is not yet relevant here, for first we must question whether selfhood can be discussed. If we can discuss existence because we exist, we cannot discuss non-existence precisely because we can discuss existence. Words are shadows of objects; where there is neither light nor objects, there are no words. We cannot see a fruit if we are blind, nor taste it if we have torn out our tongues; but even with all our senses intact we cannot see, taste, or ponder upon an unborn chick. It is ill conceived to speak of those not conceived. What if they gave a chicken barbecue and nobody came, not even the chickens?

Because both cow and calf share common stalls, our bovine companions are half as fortunate as our feathered friends. Even in the most loving of circumstances within the small family farm, cows deserve better than what winter's worst brings: barns heated only by their bodies, and walks outside the barn for but an hour a day. The calves for whom the milk is intended are confined to even less varied and more brutal existences. Humans rob the calves from the cows, and the milk from the calves. Though cows produce enough milk for both humans and calves (humans have bred them to do that), humans are greedy: all male calves and over half the females are kidnapped in the first week of birth, trucked to the veal farm where they are fattened for four months, then shipped to the slaughterhouse, then packaged for the supermarket, then purchased for the dinner table, where the fattened calves further fatten fattened humans. Of every five calves born, four end as meals of veal. Thus veal floats invisibly in everyone's glass of milk. "Got veal?"

Cows must be milked, but by the calves for whom the milk is intended. It is often argued that cows would die if left not milked. Cows also surely would die if left unfed, yet they are fed not because of humane compassion, but because of human greed. Furthermore, since bulls rarely are allowed to mingle with cows, the species would perish but for artificial insemination; yet they are conceived not because of conservation, but to maintain peak lactation. Farmers' rationalizations for incarcerating cows on the dairy farm compare with those of human hunters for shooting deer in the fall: to save them from starvation in the winter. Convenient explanations for atrocities have long been conjured by humans intent on self-delusion in self-defense of self-interest. Lacto-vegetarians are hardly different in regards to drinking cow milk. "Got milk?"

What is milk? It is not animal, yet not vegetable either. Mammal young of both carnivores and herbivores drink it, and its nutritional effect is rather close to both flesh and plants. No adult vegetarian would eat a hamburger made half of flesh just because the other half is of extender made from soy beans, yet many vegetarians drink milk. What comes from

an animal comes closer to being an animal than what comes
from a plant. For the vegetarian, that is too close for comfort;
and for the cow confined in her stall and her many calves in
their crates, that also is too close for comfort. Here it should
be noted that not only does an egg come from an animal, but
it could have become an animal.

Lacto-vegetarians generally eat everything *au lait* and often
consume more lacteal liquids than do carnivores meat and milk.
Yet milk is but blood modified by mammary glands. Some traditional Masai tribesmen still bleed milk cows at their necks and
drink both the blood and the milk. Like masturbating monks,
milk-drinking vegetarians are imitating the very thing they wish
to avoid. Their lips can be white from milk only because others'
hands are red from blood. Jack made no mistake when he traded
his cow for a handful of beans (nor when he sought the goose
whose eggs were not for eating). Cows make milk as food upon
which small cows can become big cows; calves are small, but not
all things small are calves; because humans are small compared
to cows means not that they are calves, yet they strangely try to
grow into big cows. The belief that cows' milk is made as food
for humans is as fallacious as the belief that their blood is for
humans, and the trail of blood leads directly to the belief that
their flesh is made as food for humans: it is flesh from which
flows both blood and milk. Someone might someday market
cows' tears, promoting them as a rich source of mineral salts.
Inducing cows to shed them should be no problem: they must
forever be crying over their spilled milk. "Got tears?"

The three foods nature creates solely for the sake of feeding animals are eggs, milk, and honey. Not even fruits fulfill
this sole function since they really envelope seeds of propaga-
tion, acting as gift wrap around a birthday present, at once

a disguise and a cosmetic. Not coincidentally, these three particular foods are made by the three particular animals for whom they are intended. The foodstuff of eggs is laid by the mother bird for the bird embryo also in the egg; milk is secreted by the mother mammal for the infant mammal also delivered from her; and honey, made by bees, is intended for bees. While animals adapt themselves to what they eat, milk and honey adapt themselves to the animals by whom they are intended to be eaten. Thus human milk is specifically adapted for humans, kangaroo milk for kangaroos, bat milk for bats, rat milk for rats—and cow milk for cows. Most human babies are born with an innate aversion to cow milk; but some infants immediately yearn for it. This should alert mom and dad that perhaps they mistakenly have given birth to a calf.

Cow milk contains three times more calcium than human milk. Cows develop bones first, for which all the calcium is needed; humans develop brains first. Cows may be less intelligent than humans, yet no mother cow is so simple-minded as to substitute human milk for hers. Ever since humans first were humans, their babies have been fed human milk (as is meant to be); adults have included cow milk as a small part of their diets for several centuries, but only as recently as the last two was it included in their infants' and as a large part at that. Whether this development tells more about the way adults feed themselves, or about the way they feed their children, or about the way they feed themselves as though children, is unclear; but we do know that drinking milk provides the infant child a means of growing up, and that among other mammals its consumption is infantile. "Got drool?"

These past two centuries have also seen a sharp increase in adult humans' consumption of cow milk and hence an increase in its production. Because we are now so accustomed to milk, cows are enslaved to us. Slaves earn no vacations, no leaves of absence for maternal affairs. Forced to produce milk at least eleven months a year, a cow's own tissues are depleted so that her milk might ostensibly nourish her calves. Her body becomes diseased; but rather than give her a vacation, humans give her a vaccination. Her milk becomes tubercular; but rather than put her out to pasture, humans pasteurize her milk. Many people eat everything at hand, including the hand. Those who drink cow milk, and thereby perpetuate her mistreatment, are biting that hand that feeds them; those who eat her flesh are eating the hand. But if we bite, or eat, the hand that feeds us, eventually it will stop feeding us or will feed us one more time, this last time with poison. Like the chick within the fertile egg, ethical consequences underlie nutritional considerations. No foods as much as those from animals are so controversial concerning what is unsafe and unholy. "Got guilt?"

The venerable law of karmic consequence dictates that those who in early life exploit cows and calves, later in life will be plagued by illness and disability. Raw milk is more nutritious than the sterilized supermarket version, but the stringent sanitation controls necessary for an edible raw milk drastically limit its supply. What is gained in quantity is lost in quality. Modern America guzzles so much on account of pasteurization, a process that not only eliminates the beneficial bacteria along with the bad, but destroys vitamins and renders minerals indigestible. Numerous studies link pasteurization, not milk itself, with arthritis. The factory-bred and conveyor-belt-fed cow today produces more milk during a shorter productive life span than ever before. And Americans drink more milk than ever before, yet are hardly any healthier.

Only humans suffer from the cholesterol diet-related diseases of coronary sclerosis in middle life and atherosclerosis in late life, and only humans drink milk past their infancy. Milk is also attributed as a mucus former in the human body. Some vegans contend that mucus is the cause, not the product, of the common cold. No one knows the cure for the common cold, but those who neither eat flesh nor drink milk truly know its prevention. Most lacto-vegetarians suffer more colds and flu, not fewer, compared to when they were carnivores, while most vegans seldom ever catch colds. "Got snot?"

If we were fortunate to have been breastfed, we were nevertheless weaned from our mother at one or two years of age. What of those who have yet to be weaned from the cow mother? Who would believe they matured from childhoods as humans only to develop into baby cows? Digestion of the mother's lactose, the sugar in milk, depends on secretion of the child's lactase. The majority of the non-Caucasian adult world, notably North and South American Indians, Australian and Pacific Island aborigines, Asians other than in northern India, and black Africans other than eastern, cannot digest and therefore do not drink milk. The Chinese raised cows for the past three centuries, but only for the flesh, and ate it sparingly: Asians have produced both flesh and milk from the simple soybean. Western nutritionists remain unable to explain the predominant "lactose-intolerance" because they explore the answer only in Caucasians. Some propose genetic digestive deficiencies, others acquired inabilities; the confusion is needless. The ancient Epicharmus, who said, "Only the mind can see and hear, everything else is deaf and blind," must have been deaf and blind. In this case we should listen with our stomachs. If lacto-vegetarians and carnivores alike withdraw all milk and milk products

from their diets for just one year, they, too, will lose their childish abilities to digest milk, outgrowing it as surely as we all
outgrew our mother's breast, and then her placebo pacifier.

The thought of bending down on our knees to suck at the
tit of a zebra or a donkey, or lifting up to our mouths the
nipple of a beaver or a monkey, should elicit a response of
either laughter or regurgitation. Why is it any different with
a cow, or a goat, or a sheep? Are we to equate ourselves with
the leech, but instead of sucking blood from the leg of another
human we suck milk from the tit of a cow? Not even the cow
mother drinks her own milk. Such a cow would hardly differ
from a human father drinking his own blood, which hardly
differs from a cow drinking a human mother's milk. Her calf
drinks her cow milk, but the cow herself does not. Why do the
human father and mother drink the cow's milk? Because they
also drink the calf's blood. "Got blood?"

The archetypal story of the UNICEF program during the
1950s that donated truckloads of dry milk to African children attests to the wisdom of the Third World, who used it
to whitewash walls, as well as to the cultural imperialism
and ethnocentrism of the "First." What one race of people
digest, disgusts another. Eskimos have been known to devour
so much raw flesh at a single sitting that at the end they could
not stand up; Northwest Amerindians traditionally com-
peted against one another in a variation of their potlatch with
salmon as the wealth, and each contestant destroyed by digestion as much as fifteen pounds of it cold; Tartar tribesmen
relished frozen horse flesh; and to this very day, the French
esteem fried frogs' legs and steamed snails. All of this might
be regarded by the average American beef eater as loathsome,
yet no carnivores witnessing any of the above can experience

half as much revulsion as do vegetarians in viewing their peers eating beef and burgers. "Got puke?"

Those who prefer their beef rare might be impressed by the Abyssinians who herded a cow to the kitchen door, severed small chunks of flesh from its still living body, and then engorged greedily while the animal watched from outside. A fisherman once caught a fish, cut a morsel from its side, baited his hook with the morsel, threw both the fish and his hook back into the water, and then caught the same fish. Not wishing to waste food, thrifty moms often feed the leftover flesh from the suffer [sic] table to the family dog or cat. Yet they toss it to the wrong animal and would waste far less returning it to the animal from which it came: it needs it most. The twice-caught fish obviously lacked something and did its best to retrieve what once made it whole. Those animals who must eat others' bodies do so because of a deficiency, be it nutritional or spiritual. Eating is a means of seeking companionship with the things we eat. Those who eat many animals probably are very lonely.

We have our weaknesses. When we want to be treated like everyone else, we say we are *also* human; but when we want special privileges, we say we are *only* human. And we are also only animal. Though we may or may not place animal bodies into our mouths, our mouths are nevertheless placed inside animal bodies. The path out of our bodies is a slow one. Lacto-ovo-vegetarianism, lacto-vegetarianism, and ovo-vegetarianism are steps in the right direction, and are good compromises for and concessions to those who care not to aspire higher. This is intended only to qualify "lactism" and "ovism," not to mock them, though the defenses that some vegetarians uphold against veganism sometimes sound as pig-headed as those of carnivores'. Literal statements about calf rennet in hard cheese, bone and urine in toothpaste, lard in peanut butter and pie crust, gelatin in candy, and flesh fat in soap are often responded to with disbelief. Metaphors about veal floating invisibly inside glasses of milk and about hearts beating silently inside eggs are met with blank stares of denial and doubt. "Got shame?"

Yet veganism can no more be expected of vegetarians than vegetarianism of carnivores: all that we can hope for is that we know the facts. Once learned, the facts can be gathered into two heaps: the ethical in the mind as theories, the dietetic in the stomach as recipes. More people are qualified speakers on nutrition than on philosophy since nutrition offers more answers with far less questioning. Furthermore, philosophy is of little value to the lamebrain dying of malnutrition. Little wonder that books on vegetable and vegetarian cooking outnumber those on vegetarianism one-hundred to one, and that those on vegetarianism provide more seasoning than reasoning. The word *vegetarianism* itself is short on clarity and long on syllables, hence the bestselling books on the subject shun the V word in their titles or on their covers. You are what you eat, but you become what you read. So once the facts are learned, then what; or rather, so what? They can be ignored or heeded: if heeded, they can be affirmed or denied; if affirmed, they can be used rightly or wrongly.

More good people than bad are alive but fewer right beliefs than wrong are shared by them: only one shortest line exists between two points, while infinite other longer paths surround it. A wrong belief may be based upon misguided misinformation from poison ivy league professors whose endowed chairs are funded by food industries; if so, then the believer can plead innocence. Despite the daily slaughter of innocent animals, humans who admit apathy or who even confess guilt can live on in a state almost akin to grace. Carnivorism in no way negates goodness; it simply does not let us forget evil. Some places remind us of evil more than others. In Israel, employment of teenagers is forbidden anywhere an undesirable environment might impair their physical, emotional, or moral development. Although the military somehow fails to appear on the list, included among these forbidden places are bars, mines, mental hospitals, and slaughterhouses. Kibbutzim may be small societies nearest to our Western conception of Utopia, but as long as most of them tend to their chicken coops they will remain a long way from approximating Eden. Only in Eden was there no sin and, therefore, no death and, therefore, no killing and, therefore, no flesh. The *therefore's* can easily be reversed. No matter how few animals we might eat and cause to die, we, too, still will die and be eaten. Even confused Prince Hamlet understood that we fatten fish with worms, and ourselves with fish, that we ourselves might fatten worms.

The Threefold Godhead of Hinduism—Shiva, Vishnu, and Brahma—forms the door that slams shut our small square cell called life. The individual, even in sackcloth and barefoot, allows now one head to raise itself atop the body, and now another, but always the other two remain waiting. Destruction provides the foundation for creation: we are not green, do not contain chlorophyll, cannot produce our own food, and so we do destroy plants. The closest we can come to complete harmlessness is fruitarianism (not necessarily "fruit-fruitarianism"), whereby the plant remains alive though we eat its products. Though we may chop down trees for paper on which to write and read instructions and declarations on how and why not to chop down trees, at least we destroy far less than any carnivore. The point here is that we destroy still less if we do not drink milk. Like the active member of Greenpeace and the devoted worker at the ASPCA who meet each other for lunch of burgers and fries, the vegetarian who drinks milk waits according to an obsolete timetable for the same train of thought that stops at, but goes no farther than, being a humanitarian who eats flesh. Is veganism justified? The question is answered best by the very uneasiness of the lacto-ovo-vegetarian. Is it practical? Can it be practical, can it be practiced, in modern Western society? Truth owes no homage to any society, East or West, nor to any diet, worst or best. Where there is a will, there need be no whey.

Certain books we finish reading and though we never again refer to them, we store them on a shelf. That is important; rather than discard them, we store them on a shelf. Other books we read and finish, and find so worthwhile or so confounding that we read them again. Concerning the grosser pleasures of life such as smoking, drinking, doping, gambling, carousing, and flesh eating, many come to a potential end to these youthful indulgences and indiscretions, and yet begin them again; others reach some closure that warrants no repetition, and leave them behind. This chronology of dissimulation stresses that each be cast aside one by one in its own due time, not collectively in a meaningless group ceremony, and be renounced not out of sacrifice but out of boredom. Indeed, the ascetic, as Tolstoy said, is one who derives more reward renouncing a small pleasure than indulging in it. We need not be sorry to have pursued and perused these volumes: quite the contrary, we can be glad to have opened them, and just as glad to have shut them closed. Though they are not worth rereading, we might store them for future reference in which to research a passage, or to quote from, devoting careful attention to citing our sources. What was the text becomes the epigraph and index.

It amounts to this: development is a product not of renunciation; rather, renunciation is a product of development. A projectile falling to the earth gains velocity only to a point, after which it descends at a steady speed. As great a weight that any book may add to the evidence, its plea for vegetarianism cannot prod carnivores who already are proceeding along their life's way at their own pace; likewise for veganism in relation to lacto-vegetarians. "Why then are you writing?" the reader asks. "Why then are you reading?" the writer answers. No book, not even the Gospels, is the gospel truth, so no book should be taken on the author's word. In regards to books about nutrition, we should judge only by the results: the writers' and readers' pictures of health. While we can't always tell a book by its cover, maybe we can offer prognoses of the health of writers and readers by their looks, and then compare our forecast by their looks to the content of their books. Yet readers do not necessarily put into action what they read, so let's skip their books; instead let's head to supermarkets and health food stores. We likely will see that the health of shoppers who purchase mostly fresh fruits and raw vegetables appears better than those who buy much white bread and many hot dogs. While waiting in line at checkout counters, as the cashier rings them up, we can check them out.

Beyond the marketplace, flesh is a natural food for predators who stalk and kill their prey, and for scavengers who pick clean the leftovers. And human milk is a natural food for humans, but not all humans, only those who are infants. And cow milk is a natural food for cows, but not all cows, only those who are calves. Cow milk maybe, just maybe, is a natural food for humans who are infants and who are orphans and who drink it warm in a natural manner as do calves: groveling on all fours, suckling under the udder. Cow milk is not a natural food for adult humans who shy away from any intimacy with the cow, but instead drink her milk chilled and from a glass or a bottle. Such humans display their lack of faith in food in its natural state, in which case they do not have faith in (if they are believers) God or (if they are not) Nature.

So much for talk about food; let us eat it, and be done with it. All these pages have been an invitation to dinner. You have arrived at the agreed time, and have sat down. The table is set: wooden bowls, chopsticks, cloth napkins, earthenware mugs, and candlelight. Everything appears to be ready. What is that you ask? You want to know, where is the food? What do you mean? No one told you that you were supposed to bring it? Well, good! As long as you are here, we can talk. And not about the food. For the time has come to turn to the more serious side of our subject, to matters of life and death. But we are not obligated to turn to it too seriously. Because life is a joke, and death its laughter.

PART TWO: ETHIC

It is not surprising that the lambs should bear a grudge against the great birds of prey, but that is no reason for blaming the great birds of prey for taking the little lambs. And when the lambs say among themselves, "Those birds of prey are evil, and he who is as far removed from being a bird of prey, who is rather its opposite, a lamb—is he not good?" then there is nothing to cavil at in the setting up of this ideal, though it may also be that the birds of prey will regard it a little sneeringly, and perhaps say to themselves, "We bear no grudge against them, these good lambs, we even like them: nothing is tastier than a tender lamb."

FRIEDRICH NIETZSCHE
The Genealogy of Morals,
"Good and Evil" "Good and Bad"

6.

ANIMALS AND INFIDELS

Because Christian morality leaves animals out of account, they are at once outlawed in philosophical morals; they are mere "things," mere means to any ends whatsoever. They can therefore be used for vivisection, hunting, coursing, bullfights, and horse racing, and can be whipped to death as they struggle along with heavy carts of stone. Shame on such a morality that is worthy of pariahs, and that fails to recognize the eternal essence that exists in every living thing, and shines forth with inscrutable significance from all eyes that see the sun!

ARTHUR SCHOPENHAUER
On the Basis of Morality

THE PAGES OF HISTORY are written in blood, but at least the East's blood has been mostly human. The ideologies of holy books rarely correspond with the realities of history books; the religions of both East and West preach love for humans, neither region practicing what is preached. The East has much more frequently preached love also for animals and has treated them accordingly better than has the West. And yet, and yet. Whoever compares one culture with another had better know everything about both; but who knows everything? Of all nations, India is most often cited for its concern for the cow above all animals. But it is in part a self-concern that has not much to do with animals; it is like the subdued ruthlessness of certain anti-vivisectionists who wish to abolish animal experiments only because the results rarely prove applicable to humans and when indeed applied actually prove quite disastrous. In this way, as cake in the West, India knows it cannot both eat its cows and milk them, too.

Just as the tractor is dear to the farmer and the family car to the father, the ox is holy to the rural Indian farmer and father, and the cow sacred to all because she produces both oxen and milk. Hindus react in a half-facetious manner to Western suggestions of slaughtering the cows for flesh food, but the facetiousness is underlain with grim premonitions: the farmer would eventually have no tractor, the father no car, and the mother neither fuel from their dung nor milk for her young. In the final evaluation, since the fuel is used mostly for cooking and the milk not just for weaning, the suggestions may be only half foolish, but not for the reasons Westerners intend and only so long as alternatives exist. Alas, choice is a consequence of affluence; presently rural India has not much choice. If most of that nation were carnivores, it could not support even half of its already hungry population; if everyone were free from their religion for just one year to turn the sacred cow into roast beef, the cow would become scarce and roasts would become rare. Indians would be like the Siriono, an Amerindian tribe in Eastern Bolivia; they destroyed most of their native fruit trees with their newly acquired iron tools because cutting the trees down was less an effort than climbing them.

The cow is not held so sacred as we from far away might think. A Hindu will not kill one outright but will tie an old or ill animal to a stake until she starves to death, will not slaughter a calf who competes for milk but will yoke him in such a way that his mother will not nurture him, and will not sell an ox to the butcher but will sell him to a Muslim or a Christian who will sell him to the butcher. Even within the bounds and bonds of Hinduism, the Hindu gets away with murder.

In Buddhism, all life is sacred though it exists in higher and lower forms. In Jainism, all life is sacred and equal: there are no higher or lower forms. In Judaism and its two ungrateful heirs, Christianity and Islam, there are again higher and lower forms, but only the humans are held sacred. These two latter religions of preference and prejudice have brandished their swords wherever they have spread their gospels, and have extended their missionary zeal to the dinner table: consumption of a calf and a lamb is a way of converting them into Christians and Muslims.

Western religion, and to some smaller degree Western philosophy, exclude animals from their ethics as intently as flesh cookbooks leave out telling about the screams of pain and the streams of blood that came from the steak that now so silently sizzles on the grill. From the very beginning. the Bible gives mankind dominion (domination) over all living, moving things. To what purpose? Despite mother love and other love; despite our love for our dogs who wake us from sleep to take them for walks, and our support for the ASPCA where we put to sleep our dogs whom we have tired of walking; despite humanitarians gone to Sierra Leone to medicate the poor, and gurus come to Beverly Hills to meditate the rich; despite the murals of the Sistine Chapel, and the morals of the chapel Sisters; despite the walls built by Chinese to keep out invaders, and the cathedrals built by Christians to take in the infidels; despite spaceships and satellites, and microscopes and isotopes; despite MyFace and SpaceBook social networking, and VeggieLove and ZooMatch.com wedsite dating; despite Mass, Communion, and mass communication; despite irrigation, desegregation, and group-plan hospitalization; despite all sacred scriptures and all world wisdom; despite all this, we still kill other humans in the name of foolish wars, animals in the name of faddish foods, and ourselves in the name of fame and fortune. All this to what purpose? That we, created on the sixth day, might bring the entire planet to rest on the seventh, that with either a bomb or a whimper the cycle might start again if not from the very beginning then from the roaches and the rats who survive everything.

Not much oxygen or ink need be wasted denigrating Western religion; it is dead, killed by a newer creed, science, against which we now must struggle, along with its most frequently performed, most obdurately wrong rite, vivisection. In the inhumane name of human progress, scientists torture animals instead of heretics, sacrificing lives for solutions instead of salvations. The over one hundred million annually tolled tortures have proven only that animals feel pleasure and pain and that scientists feel no pity or shame. Where religion brought intolerance and hate and called it the search for divine love, science brings suffering and death and calls it the quest for eternal life. The abolitionist battle may not be won in our lifetimes, meanwhile what we can do is use no drugs for our fetishes or cosmetics for our blemishes, nor contribute to charities and foundations that finance researchers to pour acids and dyes into the asses and eyes of a thousand rabbits to prove again and again that the rabbits will go crazy and blind and that the scientists already are.

The enigma "What is life?" will never be answered in the riddled body of a vivisected animal, and may never be answered at all. Those questions which are more reasonable to consider are "What is human life?" and "What is human truth?" The reason for human existence on earth will have to be sought in humans, indeed in ourselves. Christianity negates individual will, and instead attributes awareness of truth to divinity. Plato's Idealism propounds that we all already possess the truth but need only to be made conscious of it. Thus Christ is said to be the Truth, while Socrates' task was not even to teach the truth but to awaken it from dormancy in others.

This difference between Western philosophy and Western religion is between being wakened from sleep and being reborn from death. Yet the former is a metaphysical metaphor for the latter. So do we or do we not possess the truth? If we indeed possess it, we possessed it from the eternal beginning and shall possess it until the eternal return. But if we do not possess it, then at this very moment we are stupidly demonstrating to each other our separate silly untruths while awaiting messages if not from the Messiah, then from the Pope.

As for the Church's treatment of animals, Pope Innocent VIII during the Renaissance required that when witches were burned, their cats be burned with them; Pope Pius IX during the 19th century forbade the formation of an SPCA in Rome, declaring humans had no duty to animals; Pope Pius XII during World War II stated that when animals are killed in slaughterhouses or laboratories " ... their cries should not arouse unreasonable compassion any more than do red-hot metals undergoing the blows of the hammer"; and Pope Paul VI in 1972, upon blessing a battalion of Spanish bullfighters, became the first Pope to bestow his benediction upon the one cruelty that even the Church had condemned. The bullfights have always been held on Catholic feast days; in fact, one of the stylized sweeps of the toreador's cape is called the Veronica, as though used to wipe the tears of the bull on his way to crucifixion.

The implications for discussion of diet are these: the Pre-Socratic, Socratic and Platonic, and Neo-Platonist philosophers were generally vegetarians, whereas rabbis bless butcher knives and Rembrandt's paintings of slaughtered oxen symbolize crucified Christs, despite Christ's own command to replace flesh with bread and blood with wine. Weighing the solipsism of Idealism against the serendipity of Christianity, we must seek the tenets of philosophers and forget the canons of priests. Yet philosophers, also human, share in making mistakes. Even gods err: that Jews, Christians, and Muslims cite passages in their holy books which support carnivorism and animal exploitation means that theirs either are wrong books or wrong gods.

We by no means wish to write the history of philosophy or religion any more than of vegetarianism or carnivorism. Just as the philosophy of history is more interesting than the history of philosophy, any new philosophy of vegetarianism is more edifying than any history of vegetarianism or even history of the philosophy of vegetarianism: the truly innovative may supersede, but still includes, the tiresome old. Animals have found many friends in philosophers, several to whom are credited the epigraphic seeds scattered throughout these leaves. Nevertheless, a handful of venom-mouthed zoo-phobes have wiggled their way onto the pages of the history of philosophy. The most notorious of these is Descartes, who even practiced vivisection. Like a judge condemning a criminal whose one offense was having been born non-human, Descartes pointed to a dissected calf and said that there he found his library— and he then proceeded to burn his books. *Cogito ergo sum. I think, therefore I am.* Assuming animals could not speak, he denied that they could think, and so he doubted they could feel, and so he questioned their very existence. According to

Descartes, animals behaved without the intervention of a soul, hence without consciousness, and were machines, mere animal-automatons made of wheels and weights like clocks.

Descartes was on one of the typically Western paths of inquiry when he separated mind from matter, but then lost his footing when designating animals as all matter, and then lost his way when claiming that animals did not matter. Philosophy's pendulum swings differently every generation. Like science, but unlike religion, it does not hesitate to disavow in the morning everything it had pledged the night before. It is vanity to take credit when one is right, strength to confess when one is wrong, and wisdom to admit to one's contradictions. Thus philosophy esteems its Descartes, but also its Montaigne, whose *Apology for Raimond Sebond* posits animal instincts as surpassing our intelligence, and their stupidity our wisdom.

History rallies behind maxims, for they must be terse else easily forgotten. *I think, therefore I am* is actually a truncation of *I doubt, therefore I think, therefore I am*, which could be the battle cry of mankind's soldiers in its war against the animal kingdom. ("I kill, therefore I am" would be closer to their anthem.) As the slaughterer slits the neck of every passing chicken on the disassembly line, perhaps he thinks to himself, "I think, therefore I am; I think, therefore I am; I think, therefore I am." Or perhaps, as he slits its neck, he whispers the obverse to the chicken, "You do not think, therefore you now are not."

Cartesian logic was a blunder of philosophy. Let us leap back two thousand years to perhaps its first blunder. If greatness is commensurable with being misunderstood, the possibility must not be overlooked that we completely misinterpret Descartes. But no doubt exists that another such misconstrued thinker and thought are Protagoras and his decree, "Man is the measure of all things." History, that is, human history, would have us believe that this means that all is measured with humanity as its standard, that we are everything, that the whole of the universe in our absence amounts to nothing. This fits right into humanity's scheme of things in its subjugation of the planet, the plants, and of course the animals. Yet really we humans and all the finned, feathered, and furred are common vassals sharing the same single thin crust of earth.

Actually, the accurate translation from the Greek is not *man* but *a man*. "*A man* is the measure of all things." The additional article is crucial. The former signifies *all humanity,* while the latter specifies *a single human.* In Plato's *Theaetetus* (161c), Socrates says, "I am surprised that he [Protagoras] did not begin his Truth with the words, the measure of all things is the pig, or the baboon, or some sentient creature still more uncouth." Perception, not erudition, is the root of conception. Those who see, know. Socrates further says that if an animal also perceives it also is a measure, and then what it judges for itself is as proper as what any human judges. If each is the measure of individual wisdom "...then where is our comparative ignorance or the need for us to go and sit at his [Protagoras'] feet?" We could say that those of us with such insight could as well sit at the feet of a pig, a baboon, or a rabbit, as of Protagoras, Descartes, or even Socrates. But for others, hardly enough feet can be found. This could be the origin of carrying a rabbit's foot as a good luck charm.

Walking along a forest trail, suddenly you stop. You spot a rabbit crouched motionlessly, she having spotted you. The two actions are similar, only the intentions differ: you stop in order to see, she stops in order to avoid being seen. As she stops and stares at you, you stand and stare at her; so long as you do not move, she does not move...and you two still might be standing there and staring. She fears you because she had no evidence whether or not you were harmless. She fears you because of the bad reputation caused by the stones, slings, arrows, and guns of crazed carnivores.

A conclusion such as this will no doubt appear to the flesh eater a product of specious logic of which only the vegetarian is capable. Carnivores could protest that they are not so cruel as to stone rabbits. But just as it is contradictory for the humanitarian not to be a vegetarian, so it is for the carnivore not to stone rabbits. Anyone strolling in the woods and happening upon a patch of ripe red raspberries might not conceive of picking them because of fullness of stomach, laziness of body, hesitancy of mind at trying things new, or preference to leave the berries to the rabbits. Likewise the carnivore might not try to stone the rabbit because of fullness, or laziness, or hesitancy at trying something not wrapped in pre-priced cellophane, or preference to leave the rabbit to the hawks. Only through self-deception can a carnivore disclaim cruelty, for if someone else were to stone it, a second person to skin it, a third to cook it, and a fourth to serve it, it is clear who would be the fifth and sixth to pay for and to eat it. "We have rabbits" reads the sign on a storefront, which at first glance appears to be a pet shop, but is actually the butcher.

Strato the Peripatetic observed that without intelligence animals cannot perceive. When Dr. Kellogg of cornflake fame asked, "How can you eat anything that has eyes?" he was also asking how anyone with intelligence can eat anything that also is ruled by intelligence. An animal that has eyes (or that once had them, as in the case of cavefish, or that maintain the organ but not its function, as in the case of the blind) has a brain to convert visual perceptions into logical conceptions. Who are so blind that they cannot see that the rabbit also sees? It stares at you out of rabbit eyes, just as you stare at it out of human eyes. The hawk, too, sees the rabbit out of hungry hawk eyes, for the hawk should no more eat berries than a rabbit eat hawks. We do not expect a child to think like an adult. So why expect an animal to think like a human?

All humans think differently from one another, and animals think differently from each other and from humans. This is not disparity, but diversity. Each new thinker is merely a new scale by which to measure the world. Speech has been the mark of thought in a world where words alone offer meager proofs. The childish, the tongue-tied, the hare-brained, and the bird-brained are all the same pejoratives. Hardly enough to be just humans, we who stand up and are counted must be thinking humans. While we all potentially are omnivores, some are largely carnivores, but many more are wholly herbivores, in part because for many, necessity leaves few options other than vegetarianism. The rest of our species moderates between necessity and choice, but not all of us exercise that choice: most remain at rest in the vestibule of indecision by letting either waiters or mothers (or, in the case of some males, their other mothers, their wives) choose their dinners. Socrates says to "Know Oneself" and Kierkegaard to "Choose Oneself." Vegetarians, through thought and action, choose themselves, while the rest of the West lose themselves: the sons and the husbands by not choosing, the mothers and wives by choosing nothing new.

We do not choose between birth and death; birth and death choose us. We do choose between life and suicide. Is life worth living? Assuming the affirmative, our second query is how we should live, and our third is who should live. Mix together these improvised ingredients of inquiry into a recipe-less stone soup, cook the soup for four hours over the heated arguments concerning what food is worth eating, and in time for dinner, though it will then be served cold, we will have prepared one big question upon which to chew: "What life is worth eating?" After separating the sheep from the goats and sifting the wheat from the chaff, next we must elect whether to keep the sheep from the wheat or to mix them into the soup. This, of course, is the choice of vegetarianism, of carnivorism, or of neither, of hesitation and negation, the supreme existential condition: starvation. These developments of conscience and conscious-ness few initiate and fewer conclude. That we are alive is no testament to an affirmation of life any more than is flesh eating evidence of any negation; not killing ourselves on the one hand, and killing animals on the other, are owed neither to consent nor denial, but to ossification and superficiality. In any case the opposite of the suicide is the vegetarian, and the large numbers of each suggest a lot of people have been doing a lot of thinking.

Many people think that only people think. They have stared too long at their mirrors without mentally stepping aside to glimpse the animal within. How can they justify killing animals unless their thesis supports killing humans? Can such support truly exist? Dostoyevsky's Kirilov, in *The Possessed*, argued in support of such killing, but only for killing himself. In his mind, the suicide exalts himself into a god, into a being whose actions beckon beyond others' commands. Lucky for other humans and animals, Kirilov, once a god, could take no further life. So that they can get away with what they cannot explain away, humans who kill animals can equate themselves only with other animals. The commandment "Thou Shalt Not Kill" may or may not have been decreed about animals. It certainly was not decreed to animals. And it certainly was not related to his tribe by a prophet who practiced what he preached.

The brain is much like a gland that secretes thoughts. Carnivores who eat flesh saturated with animal hormones will think animal thoughts. Humans who eat rabbits will become either more like rabbits or less like rabbits and more like hawks that also eat rabbits. But rabbit or hawk, they become less human. Berries secrete no such thoughts; rabbits that eat berries remain rabbits, just as humans who eat berries remain humans. Under this rate of exchange, animals gain every advantage in eating humans, but humans none in eating animals. Under this rate of exchange, the only animals humans should risk eating are other humans. Under this rate of exchange, the human with better-than-average intelligence runs greater risks than does someone of lesser intellect.

That the brain is a gland that secretes thoughts is a thought first attributed to an old philosopher whom we did not have to eat to know this, but had only to read. Whether we eat him or read him, we do not have to believe him. Some people believe everything they read, some only what they read. Some will believe only what they see, or if blind, then only what they hear. Perhaps people believe animals do not think because no animal has told them otherwise. Human infants not yet cognizant of human language are certainly not denied their potential for learning it, for speaking through it, eventually for thinking through it. And dare anyone point to a mute's inability to speak as evidence of incapacity to think? Not until the 1950s did humans finally recognize that apes' vocal tracts, not necessarily their brains, are incapable of human speech. Wonders of science, and of vivisection!

Many methods of communication exist. Speech and sound are not singular. Some animals depend more on sight, others on smell, many on touch. Some fishes signal through electrical impulses; fireflies flash lights; honeybees dance. Certain animals incapable of human speech are nevertheless capable of learning human symbols. This has been demonstrated over and over again in research with chimpanzees and gorillas who have mastered hundreds of words in American Sign Language. Their statements are at times pure poetry. Washoe, the first of these chimps, coined the phrases *rock berry* for the Brazil nut and *apple which is orange* for the orange. Lucy, another ape poet of the post-beaten generation, called the hot radish *cry hurt food* and the watermelon *drink fruit*. And the caged Washoe once signaled to a sympathetic visitor, "Get me out of here!"

As is now known to be true for porpoises, dolphins, and whales, animals converse extensively in their own vocabularies. Some even sing. As philologians we must blame only ourselves for so long neglecting to learn their languages. We say in English that we need only learn French or German or Italian to love the people and cultures of France or Germany or Italy. Those who are more interested in *pâté de foie gras*, liverwurst, and salami should strive to hear the more universal cries of pain at the slaughterhouse.

Some still will deny animals their thoughts in order to deny them their lives. Until such denials cease, no rapprochement will be reached, because the concordance must be in terms not of animals' inability to speak our many languages, of which most of us speak only one, but of ours to hear and understand theirs. If we are so smart, why have we taken so long? Our lack of understanding can be attributed as much to our ears, which cannot perceive their languages, as to their tongues, which cannot intonate to speak ours. Dogs hear pitches beyond our range; dolphins both hear and emit such sounds. Dolphins understand each other and to a considerable extent understand us; some even understand we cannot understand them, for they have been known to keep their quacking and whistling within our auditory abilities when in our presence. That they understand that we do not understand them is a considerably greater accomplishment than our own understanding. Meanwhile we had better watch out. Just before he turned against the world in a rage of destruction, the monstrous product of vivisection in Mary Shelley's *Frankenstein* observed: "Sometimes I wished to express my sensations in my own mode, but the uncouth and inarticulate sounds which broke from me frightened me into silence again." If dolphins, for instance, could speak in human language, and specifically in English, perhaps the first thing they would say to us is "A Dolphin is the measure of all things." Yet they remain reticent.

In 1823, America introduced enforced silence in its prisons. Thus the land of liberty became the first to employ one of the cruelest of all punishments. Perhaps dolphins, like our silent deities, wish to punish us; or perhaps they simply do not wish to be misunderstood. Those animals that walk, all would walk barefoot like Socrates through the streets of Athens, and like Socrates they never would need to read to know themselves. The question remains whether we humans will know ourselves, for in so knowing we surely will know that we, too, are animals, and that all animals already know themselves. Meanwhile, until all-knowing animals stoop to human language, few sounds or words express more for the cause of vegetarianism than do "Oink!", "Moo!", and "Cock-a-Doodle-Doo!"

7.

CARNIVORAL DEATH
AND KARMIC DEBT

A Robin Red Breast in a Cage
Puts all Heaven in a Rage.
A dove house fill'd with doves & pigeons
Shudders Hell thro' all its regions
A dog starv'd at his Master's Gate
Predicts the ruin of the State.
A Horse misus'd upon the Road
Calls to Heaven for Human blood.
Each outcry of the hunted Hare
A fibre from the Brain does tear.
A Skylark wounded in the wing,
A Cherubim does cease to sing.
The Game Cock clip'd & arm'd for fight
Does the Rising Sun affright.
Every Wolf's & Lion's howl
Raises from Hell a Human Soul.
The wild deer, wand 'ring here & there,
Keeps the Human Soul from Care.
The Lamb misus'd breeds Public strife
And yet forgives the Butcher's knife.
He who shall hurt the little Wren
Shall never be belov'd by Men.
He who the Ox to wrath has mov'd
Shall never be by Woman lov'd.
The wanton Boy that kills the Fly
Shall feel the Spider's enmity.

The Catterpiller on the Leaf
Repeats to thee thy Mother's grief.
Kill not the Moth nor Butterfly,
For the Last Judgement draweth nigh.
He who shall train the Horse to War
Shall never pass the Polar Bar.
The Beggar's Dog & Widow's Cat,
Feed them & thou wilt grow fat.

WILLIAM BLAKE
from "Auguries of Innocence"

I T IS VERY INTERESTING to consider the lilies of the field, and also very easy; let us instead consider the wool moths in our wardrobe closets and the roaches and ants in our kitchen cabinets. If we kept our counters and cupboards completely clean, the roaches and ants would evade our detection. But one food that they relish is grease, the cooking of which splatters more than any other food. It is entirely fitting that animals that many people like most to eat should attract other little animals that most people like least to see. Likewise for the moths in our bedrooms: it is absolutely appropriate that the one species of animal that relishes our sweaters eats only its fibers made from another species of animal.

We could resort to boric acid and camphor, in which case it is entirely fitting and absolutely appropriate that what is intended in a big way to poison tiny animals such as ants and moths, will also in little increments poison large animals such as ourselves. We pay more to kill them than to let them survive, for such is the mentality of our nuclear age. Civil wars are conflicts in which the divided nation has no winners but, whether civil war or world war, both sides always suffer. When two cavalries opposed each other on the battlefield, the side that always lost was the horses. In the next world war, there will be neither winners nor losers; there will be no one.

An Irishman might feel solidarity with other Irishmen, or a Catholic with other Catholics, or an Englishman with other Englishmen, or a Protestant with other Protestants. Those who discern less ethnic or religious distinction between themselves and others, if white might identify with other whites, or if male with other males. The truly noble mind feels affinity with all humanity. Yet this, too, is limited. Why stop at humans? Should we not encompass the whole of life? And why stop at life? Albert Schweitzer's own reverence for life reached beyond the leaf that he dared not pluck to the icicle that he dared not shatter. The less unique we think ourselves, the more we sense ourselves in all that surrounds us and the more we sense what surrounds us in ourselves. Surrendering to surrounding, we should understand that two things moving along similar paths probably began from similar origins: we should realize our common bond with animals, all animals, not just the butterflies but also the moths, not just the rabbits but also the rats. To fail to do so, and to fail to teach our children to do so, will cause the younger generation to fail to recognize its common bond with us, its older generation. Those who see no further than their own egos and the egos' barricades, their bodies, imitate Thyestes, burying their teeth in their own flesh as they delude themselves that it is the flesh some other animal. Humans should acknowledge their debt to the animal kingdom; but rather than pay them back, humans eat them up.

A large part of the human world, the part that eats few or no animals, believes in the concept of transmigration of souls, which instructs that people who kill animals will be reborn as animals to suffer the same death. But time, reaching into infinity yet disregarding continuity, knows no waiting: humans destined to return as those animals are at once the animals killed and the humans killing them. "This thou art; all is one." We are all one; but, like two casual acquaintances at a restaurant, we are billed separately. We who break free from the bondage of our own passions recognize ourselves in the objects of our passions, recognize ourselves as objects of others' passions, and finally recognize ourselves and others as the passion itself. We who break from the bondage of passion, demonstrate our freedom in one way: compassion.

Karma means *action*. The Eastern law of karma might be defined in various Western ways: scientifically as action and reaction, epistemologically as cause and effect, biblically and botanically as sowing and reaping, and even economically as supply and demand. This law is enforced not by the temporal justice of a temporary nation, but by the eternal justice of the cosmos. No angel sits in Heaven calculating crimes soon to be punished when the offenders approach their personal nemeses; rather, punishments are administered the moment the crimes are committed. We need believe neither in the omnipresence of the biblical God nor in the *pasas* of the Vedic Varuna to see that the killing of an animal in even the darkest corner of the deepest cave does not escape notice: the animal sees by the same dim light as does its killer. Killer and killed, tormentor and tormented, eater and eaten, sheep and shepherd and slaughterer, are one. The predator that pursues its prey is no less compelled than its victim that flees. The dog chasing the squirrel is hardly different than the dog chasing its own tail. Victim suffers by being harmed, assailant by simply being. Nature is undeniably cruel and life unmentionably cheap, but one way we can rise above life is by not taking it.

We wander from one life to the next, and meanings meander from one word to another: metempsychosis, palingenesis, transmigration, and reincarnation all essentially mean the same. Whether we know or believe their meanings, we need investigate neither from the next life nor into our past lives to discern that among the misfortunate are those who cause that very misfortune to others. Maybe as many teeth are broken on bones in fish as on pebbles in lentils, but certainly more fishers are lost at sea than are irrigators to alligators. Maybe as many hunters as harvesters are struck by lightning, but certainly more hunters die of gunshot than do harvesters of sunstroke. Maybe as many butchers' fingers as lumberjacks' are hacked by their own axes, but certainly butchers contract more sickness and boils from the blood on their hands than do lumberjacks from the soil on their lands. And when people choke to death on what they eat, what makes them meet their end most is an end of meat.

While eating fruit is the obverse of eating flesh, the inverse of eating animals is being eaten by animals. Two thousand years, counted backwards or forwards, matter little to our present moment in human history. Two millennia ago, a few Christians were thrown to fewer lions; now many lambs are thrown to many more Christians. Humans with lamb chops in their choppers will have to wait forever for the day when "The wolf shall dwell with the lamb, and the leopard shall lie down with the kid...and the lion shall eat straw like the ox" (Isaiah 11:6-7). The angry prophet somehow failed to mention that humans, too, must sit in peace with the lamb, the kid, and the ox. While no wolves, leopards, or lions could exist in the wild if there were no deer, gazelles, or zebras, neither would lambs, kids, and calves exist on the farm if there were no farmers. If there were no farmers or farms, instead there would be much wilderness and therefore many wild animals. Nevertheless, carnivores attempt to defend the slaughterhouse by suggesting that, if not destined to die, the farm animals would not have lived. Such lecher logic of Stoic reductionism is typical of those whose chief concerns are that they themselves remain well fed upon well-fed animals. This is not humanitarianism but premeditated murder.

While many carnivores will defend flesh as a proper food, none can defend murder as a proper deed. Proper food is necessary for a healthy body and brain, and proper thoughts are needed to dwell within them. Who can defend murder as a proper thought? If our killing a cat who was about to kill a bird could be justified with the defense that we saved the life of the bird, then we could justify the cat's killing the bird who was about to kill a fly, whereby we could no longer justify our killing the cat. The point is that no human is capable of such broad vision as to be able to determine who should live and who should die. As it is, our judgments usually depend not on what criteria we contemplate, but on those we eliminate. Two people see a steak: one thinks of the mushrooms that go on top of it, and then eats the steak; the other thinks of the murder that goes into it, and then eats only the mushrooms.

The Buddha prohibited slaughtering an animal but not necessarily eating an animal. Thus carnivorism was to be tolerated so long as the animal died of its own accord. Though he disparaged both killing and eating flesh, the difference is not disparate enough; many Buddhists today are carnivores. But the Buddhism that developed after Buddha is no more the responsibility of Buddha than is contemporary Christianity the responsibility of Christ. Buddha and Christ are one, but Buddhism and Christianity are quite another. In the East, the traditional eating utensils are chopsticks, pieces of wood that hardly differ from the very vegetables they dispense; in the West, they are knives and forks, pieces of cold steel that rip and puncture flesh like nails of the crucifix. Christianity speaks of the unknown world of afterlife awaiting only humans, Eastern religions of this known world of rebirth awaiting all animals. The torment of eternal damnation in Hell is an idea inborn only of a religion whose society has built the slaughterhouse and concentration camp, and whose little children believe equally in Santa Claus as in Satan. Little wonder Hindus view existence in this world as the worst imaginable hell. Our Western assumption that life is worth all its pain and sorrow is one with which Hindus and Buddhists would not agree, but their detachment from suffering does not cause undue callousness. Conversely, Western attachment certainly has not cured it.

Judeo-Christian belief in human dignity begins in Genesis, where we are told we were made in God's image, but nowhere do we read that animals were made in humans' own image. How then can we analogize ourselves as gods to animals, giving and taking lives as we please? To seek the root of carnivorism in the West, we might seek the root of Christianity: Judaism. Moses the messenger brought down from the mountain the decree *Thou shalt not kill.* Period. While coveting refers specifically to a neighbor's spouse, or honoring to one's parents, prohibition against killing is not specific: it says simply and purely not to kill. The Ten Commandments were too demanding. His people could not uphold the Law, so Moses gave them a hundred less difficult ordinances: for instance, allowing them to kill animals so that they should at least not kill humans, permitting them to eat "clean" beasts but not "unclean." This contrasts with Seventh-Day Adventist Christianity, which considers all animals unclean; thus half its adherents are vegetarians.

A kosher Jew is furthermore forbidden to eat an animal, even one from a "clean" family, that has died on its own accord (Deuteronomy 14:21); whereas, a Buddhist is allowed *only* such an animal. But what is really being prohibited by Judaism is to eat an animal that has lived on its own accord. A kosher Jew is also forbidden the blood of an animal (Leviticus 17:12, and elsewhere), so kosher killing today entails evangelistic evisceration of the larger blood vessels by cutthroat butchers. But no matter how much they drain, blood does remain. They can no more squeeze all blood out of a carcass than squeeze any blood out of a stone. This might be read as a message, admittedly apocryphal and certainly esoteric, that *kosher kill*, like *humane slaughter*, is yet another contradiction of adjective with noun. We do not speak about Judaism as anti-Semites, nor about Christianity as outraged Jews, but about Judaism and Christianity from the viewpoint of slaughtered animals.

Chicken soup might be certified kosher, yet no hen has announced publicly her conversion to Judaism. Great pains are taken by human housewives to keep a carnivorous home kosher, but these hardly compare to the greater pains inflicted on animals in suffering a kosher death. For a few thousands of years, the kosher method of slaughter remained the most humane. But modern science has devised still more efficient and more merciful means, which religion, in its last death throes, refuses to recognize. Although less than five percent of the flesh in the United States is sought as kosher, as much as forty percent of animals are slaughtered as such. Is it a coincidence that the Book of Leviticus advises how to contend with leprosy and plague directly after its instructions of which animals to sacrifice and how to eat them? Yet use and misuse of Biblical passages are not an honest means of proof for any argument. For every passage which supports vegetarianism, another justifies carnivorism. Schopenhauer offers both at once. In *On the Basis of Morality* (section 7 of chapter 9) and *Parerga and Paralipomena* (chapter 177 of volume II), he outlines carnivorism's origin out of that ancient book of eternal ambiguity and thereby argues against the validity, not of vegetarianism, but of the Bible. For our own epoch, the Bible is a shining mirror that reflects the images of whoever gazes into it, tired of their empty echoes against the blank walls of philosophy.

The search for dubious reasons never truly justifies what we believe since we already were believers without those reasons and will continue in those beliefs, reasons or no. At best these reasons are erected as pretty facades to entice others to enter the houses in which we were born and in which we probably shall die. Such is the case in reference to the Biblical passages quoted throughout these pages: they hardly lend support, but act only as embellishments. Sometimes, keeping in mind the right reasons, we still persist in doing the wrong things; or we do the right things, but for totally wrong reasons. Then there are the wrong things done for the wrong reasons. If a carnivore might have the right to kill an animal, who can even consider it a right to consume it who has not killed it? Quite the opposite, some humans excuse their eating the animal precisely because some other human killed it. They hardly differ from patrons of stolen merchandise who rationalize their means of acquisition by saying someone else had stolen it.

Many humans do kill what they eat. In Italian towns, chickens with tied feet and geese with clipped wings are sold live in farmers markets, carnivoral carnivals. One sale between two old women was observed to last fifteen minutes before the negotiation was concluded, during which the buyer clutched the chicken by the legs, several times unknowingly and uncaringly banged its head against the ground, weighed it while yanking it to and fro, and finally dumped it into her sack. Then she must have forgotten something, pulled the chicken out again, but only halfway, stuck its legs into the railings of a nearby fence, left it dangling undoubtedly with broken legs, and then the elderly woman walked away, hunch-backed and limping. Either she abused all her chickens out of spite or she only later in life grew bent as a consequence of the chickens who, once eaten, could easily return her abuse.

When a dog bites a stranger, who is at fault? The stranger for intending to pet it? The dog for not trusting strangers? The owner for training the dog not to trust strangers? Or society for forcing owners to train dogs not to trust strangers? *Beware of Dog* signs are quite superfluous when accompanied by the bark of a dog, but the dog itself is an excessive safeguard when announced by the more congenial sign *Beware of God*. Yet both our guard dogs and our gods' dogmas are powerless puppets whose paws and laws are manifestations of karmic consequence. With open eyes, an unprejudiced mind, a clear conscience, and a rudimentary understanding of metaphysics, we can welcome all life's tragedies. None need sing the Vedic hymns or recite the Book of Job to perceive that a cause lurks behind every effect, and that another effect waits ahead of that first one. Just as zoos are animal prisons, slaughterhouses are prisoner-of-war camps in humanity's endless war against animals: hence the setting for Vonnegut's novel about American POW's in the German *Slaughterhouse Five*. A still closer link is forged between slaughterhouses and concentration camps, where human inmates were herded like sheep, carted like cattle, and slaughtered like animals. One concentration camp in fact was located near a slaughterhouse and sausage factory, perhaps so that the odor from the ovens of the camp might be mistaken for the stench of the slaughter or of the sausage. Upon liberation, the camp survivors who wandered off in search of food came first to the sausage factory. Despite the pleas of temperance from a vegetarian among them, some gorged themselves so fully that one died from the sausage. He survived the concentration camp, but not the sausage factory.

The American Army liberated Buchenwald on April 11, 1945. When will it free the inmates of America's own animal Auschwitzes? Western religions long ago ceased animal slaughter at the altar, but not yet at the abattoir. Signs outside historic Roman churches remind tourists to act respectfully since we after all are entering a place of worship. But why should we conduct ourselves any differently in than out? Why not a whole world of worship? What we would never consider doing inside, we should attempt outside. Who would kill a calf in a cathedral? On the other hand, if trees grew in churches or if services were held in orchards, we need never think twice about picking fruit from their branches. Either the chick pecks from inside its oval shell and is born, or it waits to be cracked from the outside and dies in the prying mouth of a predator or in the frying pan of a human. Although established Western religions offer little encouragement for vegetarianism, we need not go to India in search of reasons or ways. If we should decide to go, on the way we will see in Spain bulls slowly speared to death; in Italy, children playing with their food, who had strength enough only to half sever the neck of the still living chicken with whom they are playing; in Greece, kids bleeding away in the rear of butcher shops while their legs are led away in the front of the shops by customers satisfied with the freshness of the flesh; in Turkey, fish scaled while still alive...and we have not yet crossed the bridge into Asia.

We may like to think of Hinduism as synonymous with vegetarianism; in fact, barely half of all Hindus are vegetarians, and some have reverted even to animal sacrifice. Few answers can be found in India that cannot be found in Indiana, providing we provide questions. If answers cannot be found in ourselves, they will hardly be found at all. A mosque, temple, or church signifies neither less than the actual practices of its congregants nor more than the teachings of its scriptures. Vegetarianism may lack a concrete house of worship, but to its credit it also lacks the slaughterhouse; and it does have its congregants who also have their books, though sometimes these are only cookbooks.

Physically, a holy place is just a pile of bricks cemented with mortar. Lay a pile of bricks one atop the other, and you have a wall; set four such walls together, add a roof, and you have a house, a house of bricks. The bricks remain individually visible within the wall, and will remain visible again as a pile long after the wall collapses. Eat a dozen apples day after day and you have built another sort of house of worship, a human body, a body from apples, not of apples. The apples disappear right inside of your very eyes, never again to be seen. The body does not become apples; the apples become body. Just as conquerors in an occupied land naturalize the population by compulsory conversion to a new religion, required learning of a new language, and even forced feeding of a new food, so does the body overcome food by digesting food to become body. Given the choice of battling a lion, a lark, or a leek, least harm comes to everyone by combating the leek. External conflicts fought with tooth and nail parallel those internal fought with tooth and intestine. Cannibals ate only their enemies.

As in an ambush by an army, the moment food enters the mouth it is surrounded by the body in its struggle to sustain itself in the face of foreign bodies. Similarly, from the day a new pair of shoes is worn, the feet form blisters to protect the skin against the untamed skin of another animal until the leather at last attains the shape of the foot; this is called *breaking in.* The struggle between what is shoed is the same as between what is chewed; if an allergic reaction develops, this is called *breaking out.* Like a rocket shot straight up into the air which, before plummeting, for a suspended second remains totally still, eater and eaten momentarily become one. Once ingested and until digested, food is foreign matter; the more complex the food, the greater the task the body has digesting it. We already know that an animal is more complex than a plant, that flesh takes four hours to be digested but fruit only one. Physically, a kilogram of flesh equals a kilogram of apples, but digestively flesh lays far heavier on the stomach as it was transformed from ten kilograms of apples like magic. Abracadaver!

Since flesh food is plant food already transformed into an animal, might not one animal body prove most suitable as food for another animal body? The proposition would be correct if animal digestion were a process of simple assimilation. Rather, food is broken down until the source is no longer recognizable; then the simple substance is rebuilt into a different but complex material, namely the animal body. Plant food,

resisting the animal eater least, is thus more readily transformed. The body that consumes flesh produces much mucus
as protection from digesting itself in trying to digest something that is nearly the same as itself. No people literally eat
their own hearts out, but in cases of ulcers this is exactly what
they do to their stomachs. Such nourishment does not sustain
life for very long.

All life, plant and animal, depends on air and water.
Animals devour food from plants directly or from animals
that in turn devour plants, but only rarely from animals that
in turn devour animals. In any case, animals cannot do too
much with the inorganic minerals and the immaterial light
on which plants depend. Rooted in the soil and reaching
toward the sun, plants render the inorganic into organic and
the immaterial into material. What is life? Rays of light and
heaps of dust.

One way to see the light is to eat it. "Fruit bears the closest
relation to light," wrote Bronson Alcott, the transcendental-
ist friend of Thoreau. Bircher-Benner wrote that plants are
biological accumulations of light and that nutritional energy
is thus organized sunlight. His sanitarium near Zurich is quite
near to Rudolf Steiner's Goetheanum near Basel. And Steiner
wrote that the two products of animal digestion of plant foods
are inner warmth and inner light. "Turn the spotlight inward,"
said Gandhi. People can be greedy over land or gluttonous
over food growing on it, but light seldom is in short supply.
"Light! More light!" were Goethe's last words from his death
bed.

8.

THE ILLOGIC OF THE ECOLOGIC

The change which would be produced by simpler habits on political economy is sufficiently remarkable. The monop-olizing eater of animal flesh would no longer destroy his constitution by devouring an acre at a meal, and many loaves of bread would cease to contribute to gout, mad-ness, and apoplexy, in the shape of a pint of porter, or a dram of gin, when appeasing the long protracted famine of the hard-working peasant's hungry babies. The quan-tity of nutritious vegetable matter consumed in fattening the carcass of an ox would afford ten times the sustenance, undepraving indeed and incapable of generating disease if gathered immediately from the bosom of the earth.

PERCY SHELLEY
"A Vindication of Natural Diet"

ONE WAY TO MAKE ENDS MEET is to make meat end. Besides a cruelty, carnivorism is a superfluity. Like nicotine and alcohol, like caffeine and cholesterol, it is nei-ther missed nor misused by those who never use it. The world economy would advance significantly if the growing seasons and growing pains devoted to the brewing of nutritionally nil mate, coffee and tea; to the fermentation of subsequently ersatz barley, wheat, and hops; to the burning of marijuana and tobacco; and to the sterilization of sugar and whitening of wheat, were all redirected to the cultivation of real food. In these terms, flesh is only half real: a hectare of trees whose fruit is fed directly to people will fill far more hungry human mouths than a hectare of grass whose grain is fed to cattle whose flesh is fed to people. Since a moral issue matters less in picking tea leaves, harvesting hops, curing tobacco, or cutting cane, compared with slashing the throat of a lamb, the roots of vegetarianism reach deeper still, in fact all the way to the other side of the world. While Mary had a little lamb, and a little beef, and a little ham, another little girl in Africa, and a third young child in Asia, ate next to nothing.

Chickens maintain a pecking order that they arrange and rearrange whenever fed. Sometimes they peck more than feed. Humans also have a pecking order wherein the Western world feeds half on flesh while half the Eastern world half starves. The northern Arctic supports almost total carnivores, while in the tropics flesh food is far less widely known. But humans are ruled more by economy than geography. The wealthy in all societies eat more protein; the wealthy in wealthy societies eat more flesh. In continental China, high Party officials are nicknamed "Those who eat flesh."

Looking at the chickens, we see a small bird chased away from some favored feed by a large bird. Then the large bird chases yet another away, and five more small chickens begin to peck at the unguarded feed. Enough is there for all seven; but no, the large one chases each away; one by one; by the time she is alone, the feed is gone. Wanting more than her share, she guards more but loses all. So shall it happen with humans. A world war might someday be fought over oil: if not the kind poured into motors, then the kind into mouths. Alternatives exist. For instance, Albert Schweitzer in *The Ethics of Reverence for Life* tells the story of the crippled sparrow unable to compete with the flock for crumbs. So by mutual agreement, the other sparrows left untouched those crumbs nearest it. Meanwhile Westerners continue to usurp their lion's share of the pork barrel.

Hortatory oratory against stomaching torture along with nurture is a dietary objection aimed at replacing animals and animal products with plants and plant products. Yet plants, too, are alive and sense pain, so if we are to avoid moral inconsistency we can aim at eating only products of plants, not plants themselves. Samuel Butler, in *Erewhon*, wrote a convincing chapter on vegetarianism, entitled "The Views of an Erewhonian Prophet Concerning the Rights of Animals," and followed it with a countering chapter concerning not carnivorism but the rights of vegetables. It is not known whether the pain sensed by ten trees equals that felt by one cow, or even whether any such pain can be measured. But let us not give scientists any ideas for more research-and-destroy missions.

As a form of sustenance that does not grow from the ground but falls to the ground, fruit is possibly inadequate for many frozen in habits whose ice no thawing wind can melt, and it is possibly ill-advised for inhabitants of northerly cold climates. In the latter case, ripe fresh fruits in February are relatively scarce in the marketplace. While in the middle of Manhattan melons from South America can be bought in the middle of winter, this does not take into account those who cannot afford the melons, or the fact that if melons were more important than money, neither is more important than health: we might be eating some of the best food but would still be breathing some of the worst air. Now those New Yorkers who worry about getting foods wholesale as well as whole might consider moving to Los Angeles; although its air is worse, at least its fruit is fresher and cheaper. This migration indeed appears to be the trend, though many decades will have to pass before New York becomes a city solely of carnivores. Likewise, an entire population's transition from carnivore to vegetarian would be just as gradual. Even if everyone renounced flesh overnight, initially the uneaten farm animals would continue eating plants, but eventually would die and not be replenished since no farmer will invest in a supply that has lost its demand. Once gone, their unborn offspring would burden no one, and proud farmers could no longer solicit us to swallow their pride.

The ultimate knowledge of life is this: to desire nothing. Those who desire nothing out of life neither lust for life nor yearn for death; they arrive unconcerned, they depart uncaring. They try neither to forget nor to remember that out of which they appeared, nor that into which they shall disappear. They confront the void but need never fill it with pretty trinkets and petty triumphs of everyday existence. Neither do they want their own life nor do they discard it, nor do they want or discard anyone else's. Many monks eat fish, but most eat no flesh. Carnivorism contrarily is the want of others' lives by those who want more than their own. From Sophocles to Heine, from Schopenhauer to Kierkegaard, from the Upanishads to Ecclesiastes and the Book of Job, the same thought has been repeated: sleep is good, death is better, never having been born is best. But we must distinguish between dying and killing. No father claims the right to drive his daughter to her tomb just because he had delivered her from her mother's womb. The farmer who artificially inseminates the cow cannot claim the right to incarcerate the calf. It is better that the cow and her calf never exist than that they endure the misery of the slaughterhouse. Life's quality must not be sacrificed to mere quantity. The fewer farm animals eaten by humans manifests as fewer plants eaten by farm animals; by killing fewer animals we therefore kill fewer, not more, plants. "The lips of the righteous feed many" (Proverbs 10:21). But, for several reasons, we must hesitate before emphatically advocating the ecological argument.

First, if somehow the world were turned upside down, if somehow north became south, right wrong, truth falsehood, good evil, and waste parsimony, if somehow outer economics were reversed, if somehow the vegetarian diet usurped more protein land than the carnivorous, inner ethics would still obligate us to eat like pigs rather than to eat pigs. Hence detailed discussion of this aspect of the subject is unwarranted, especially since the popular paperback on vegetarianism, *Diet for a Small Planet*, elucidates this issue quite conclusively, indeed almost exclusively.

A second objection to the ecological argument is that an entirely different conclusion can be drawn from its premises: not so much to omit flesh but to reorient the diet to depend primarily on yeast and algae as protein foods. Since the consideration here is of land use, not life loss, the most worthy diet under this circumstance is one that requires almost no land. Yummy yeast and gummy algae are two such foods, seldom grown and little known.

Third, if the wasteful growing of condiment and crap crops were curtailed, carnivorism might continue for another century with the world economy unaltered. But no, ours is a society intent on shoving a cigarette in everyone's right hand and an alcoholic drink in everyone's left, so that no one has a hand free with which to do anything else. Meanwhile, growing a marijuana plant is still illegal in many places, while killing a farm animal is not.

The fourth objection is that the land-ration rationale is rooted in the same selfishness as prohibiting human cruelty to animals only because it might foster human cruelty to humans. Some neighbors help extinguish fires only for fear they might spread to their own homes. Where life is dedicated to life, then equality is established not just by elevating animals but by demoting humans. While we await the Copernicus to teach us that the earth does not revolve around ourselves, the ecological argument tries to convince us that animals are our enemies because they eat so much of our food. The tenuous tenet of *Diet for a Small Planet*, "lacto," "ovo," and "pisci" at that, is that for every human feeding off the fat of the lamb, which in turn feeds off the food of the land, at least three vegetarians can feed directly off the food of the land. The planet might, indeed, support three times its present human carnivore population if it turned vegetarian, but someday when that population reached three times itself...then what? We can only conjecture what further adjustments will have to be made, for what is offered is only postponement, not atonement.

The fifth and final drawback sprouts from the fourth. If a healthful vegetarian diet prolongs life, the many more people alive will also be living much longer. Fewer deaths result in more mouths to feed, so the ecological premise is futile in not being fatal. Small potatoes for a small planet logically finds its fruition in Swift's "Modest Proposal," unless it restricts itself both morally and orally to a diet for a planet of the apes.

The five above contentions to the ecological question are not above dispute, and unfortunately their relevant documentary evidence is meager and vague. Nevertheless, the entire issue, despite all the scientific data on its side, can hardly be the most important reason for vegetarianism since it is essentially oriented toward humans. Though not to be disregarded, it is only an ornament added to the holiday tree and is hardly cause for celebration in itself. That tree's roots reach far deeper than the "six feet under" that society digs after most of our lifetimes, for that tree is the tree of life, the whole of life, and the whole of life includes death. Our concerns are after all over matters of life *and* death. If we were to take the ecological position to its extreme, we would eat nothing so that others could eat something. Indeed, any argument for vegetarianism can be extended as well for starvation, but then so could any reasons for carnivorism be extended for cannibalism. Some who scoff at all our ideals sometimes point out that Hitler was at times a vegetarian; but at times so were this century's three great humanitarians: Gandhi, Schweitzer, and Einstein. Had Hitler not been even a sporadic vegetarian, perhaps concentration camp ovens would have produced not just soap, but soup. Where people are treated like animals, they can very easily be eaten like animals. Fortunately, Hitler did not often eat animals.

We kill to live, but the less we kill the more we live. Green plants, blessed, are free of all ill karma, but green is seen in animals only in the eyes. Deprived of chlorophyll, we choose between either killing ourselves that others might live or killing others that we might live, and then in degree for whatever choice. Or we can completely wash our hands of the matter and a million microbes known only to the gods are mercilessly dumped down the drain like so many Satans hurled from heaven. While washing their hands in preparation for vivisection, few scientists lament their million human guinea pigs and none their million million guinea pig guinea pigs. We kiss guinea pigs and gerbils as pets, but kill mice and rats as pests. We consider squirrels friendly and cuddly, but rats filthy and ugly. Is the difference in the texture of their tails or in the teller of their tales? Unable to protect wild animals from shotguns and traps, instead we protect ourselves with blindfolds and earplugs. The produce vendor shouts the price of corn but never whispers stories of the raccoon hunt the month before: in one night by a full moon three hunters and their twenty-four dogs stalked forty raccoons up six trees, and within a month all the raccoons became coonskin hats and coats, all because raccoons eat corn, too.

Though no referendum was held at the polls nor our donations sought at the street corner, we all contribute to the hunt merely by living in a society that has neither outgrown nor outlawed its L. L. Bean hunting gear. The predatory nature of primitive humans cannot be denied. Our species' few indigenous tribes that survived into the 20th century all seem to have been gatherer-hunter societies; even a small contingent of 21st century Westernized imposters, disguising themselves with the euphemism *sportsmen*, pose as predators. Their anachronistic actions turn an otherwise deadly serious affair into a game, for many do not eat what they kill. Thus some hunters might be vegetarians, though only hypothetically: vegetarianism is concerned not merely with eating and not eating, but with killing and not killing. Team sports are essentially surrogate hunts involving two tribes in competition for the "game." Hence the "pigskin" in football. Meanwhile, less active males, inclined to predation despite their sedation, recline on Sunday sofas, lackadaisical as lions after a kill, guzzling beer and gobbling hero-less sandwiches, and watch others' games distantly on television. Thus the hunt persists.

Raccoons could be poisoned or trapped, but are more often hunted. Along with deer, they are chief competitors among larger mammals on the farm for our crops. This makes them the most like ourselves, so "Man" (remember the terrifying villain in Disney's *Bambi*?) hunts them with the same weaponry he most often employs to kill others of his own species. When we aim to kill larger numbers of people we do so with larger calibers of guns: cannons and mortars and missiles. We have certainly evolved as drastically in warfare as in dinnerware: the same technology which produced the atomic bomb has brought us the microwave oven. Our military armaments in many ways reflect our dietary developments. Mammals in general began first as insect eaters like their reptilian forebears; a rare few have survived as insectivores, while the others became herbivores, nearly complete carnivores, or omnivores; a rarer few were then transformed a second time, for instance, humans from herbivores to carnivores. Only humans among all other species of mammals changed yet again, beginning as reptilian insectivores, progressing to primatial herbivores, evolving to simian carnivores, and so far concluding as omnivores, which dubiously if not deviously, but anyhow bluntly, have here been spoken of as carnivores. Anthropologists view this third step from carnivore to omnivore as one of the great changes that makes us distinctly *human*. Either this change is not great enough, or, if it is great, we are preparing for a fourth and greater change to distinguish us as *humane*: omnivore back to herbivore.

Among the five surviving species of Great Apes, three are herbivores. The fourth species, chimpanzees, when stressed for food sources do infrequently resort to consuming small yummy rodents; and presently the few remaining chimps in the little remaining wild all are stressed for food. But only the dark fifth species, humans, became routinely carnivore. The whole of our history as carnivores is short, and as omnivores shorter still, compared to other developments of ourselves and of other animals. Whereas other animals would have waited to acquire fangs and claws to become carnivores, humans simply devised clubs and spears. As humans we have some independence from the body; for gathering food, we rely not on a sneak attack but on a charge card. Like buyers on credit who have few problems returning merchandise since they have not yet paid for it, our hasty evolution actually makes for an easier return to complete herbivorism since our bodies are still designed for it. Yet, some will always find excuses for going shopping and buying "stuff," whether they need stuff or not, so the best prevention for them just may be to stay home. Likewise for carnivores: the best prevention for them just may be to stay home inside their bodies and to find no flesh in their supermarkets. If people ate raccoon flesh, the killing and the eating would not be the issue here; rather, the consideration would be the three hunters and their twenty-four dogs killing the raccoons for them.

Raccoon hunts or no, most vegetables and fruits are chemically sprayed, so everyone kills insects. No one can wash leaves clean of all their aphids or pick grains clear of all their larvae; thus those who eat organically and so do not eat insecticides, instead eat insects. Whether we kill the insects and eat the plants, or kill insects and eat insects, the road of return from omnivore to herbivore leads to yet another return: herbivore back to insectivore. Or we might even attempt to live on the organic material in mud, as does the earthworm. Beyond vegetarianism, beyond veganism, beyond fruitarianism, beyond insectivorism, we can try to live on sunshine, air, and water. Try as we might to settle at eating only fruits and killing no plants, we will still kill insects. It should be emphasized that establishing our dietary history presents many knotty problems, and not all scholars of this study have arrived at the same conclusions. This admittedly recondite reasoning for insectivorism is perhaps as sterile as fruit from the fumatory; if so, we can ponder only so far until answers elude our comprehension. Can vegetarianism be considered truly a step beyond? Beyond what? And how can it be proved so? It is not just at the dinner table that vegetarians set themselves apart from carnivores. Vegetarians who have returned to carnivorism have admitted to feeling a part of the rest of humanity again. But the point is precisely to feel unity with not only humanity, but with the whole of nature.

Natural food stores are often named The Good Earth, Down to Earth, and Back to Nature, or combinations thereof. Getting back to nature corresponds more with cutting out flesh than cutting into it because few farm animals are fed completely organically. As with the natural foods diet, the raw foods regimen is also generally vegetarian since few Westerners devour flesh raw. At first all our foods, ranging from fruits and nuts to grubs and worms, were eaten raw. Humans probably first cooked only as carnivores. Since cooking vegetables is a practice probably borrowed from cooking flesh, once we have ceased eating flesh, we should stop cooking altogether. Nevertheless, certain cooking systems such as macrobiotics do benefit their adherents, so we must approach raw reasoning with a grain of kelp seasoning. The ecological responsibility claimed for eating plants rather than animals must also be asserted for eating the same plants raw rather than cooked. We need and therefore eat far less of a vegetable raw than cooked because, when eaten raw, we get more. Flesh roasted over grills half feeds flames, just as vegetables boiled in water half nourish drains. But a sun-ripened fruit that never is tested by trials of fire and water offers itself fully to us, so long as we approach it with the tooth, the whole tooth, and nothing but the tooth. Some primitive tribes represented God by the sun and the Devil by fire. Contemporaneously we represent rationality by radiancy.

Prometheus, who gave humans fire, must also have taught what to do with it, for instance, how to use it to render flesh more pleasing to the taste. He was punished for this by having his vitals eternally devoured by vultures. Shelley tells us these vultures are metaphors for disease. This explains then the enervation of generations of our ancestors who, chained to the rock of salt, have been frying and boiling and baking and broiling, and have had problems equally with their livers as with their lives. Two marks of our human evolution were made when we cooked flesh and planted seeds. We might evolve higher by not cooking flesh and again planting our own seeds, and higher still by not eating flesh and not cooking seeds. Most of us are urbanites, so growing our own food is nearly as impossible as living our own lives. Urbanite or not, anyone can sprout seeds, grains, and smaller beans, and eat such sprouts raw. Just as more food is provided from grain fed directly to humans than from the same grain fed to cattle, who are fed to humans, and just as more nutrition is available from vegetables served raw than cooked, far more food and nutrition are gotten from sprouted seeds, grains, and beans than from not sprouted. We might not necessarily grow the sprouting seeds, but neither do the apple farmers whose groves were sowed by Grandpa Johnny.

Lao-tse said unawareness of the feet is the sign of a pair of shoes that fits, and of the waist of a belt that fits; so should we say unawareness of the body is the criterion of a diet that fits. The giant redwoods live for hundreds of years, and if they have any one role in the web of life it is photosynthesis. The human body is a temple whose walls must be buttressed as strong as the mighty redwood. Thus its single congregant might find long refuge for the years necessary to fulfill its real single goal: understanding. Perhaps, for some, vegetables are not as palatable raw as cooked, but to whom is the body as pleasurable diseased as healthy? Growing our own food teaches patience and gratitude, hence humility, and assures freshness and wholesomeness, hence health. When a raja who had ruled thousands of Asian Indians aspired to become lord over solely himself, he retired to a small plot of his former estate and ate only those foods grown with his own hands. Not all of us own land for gardens, but most have window sills and cupboards where we can grow our own sprouts. "He who cultivates barley," sings the Zoroastrian hymn, "cultivates righteousness." Thomas Jefferson understood this in intending to frame his nation's future around the farmer. Monks will often spend as much time tending their gardens as their souls, and shamans in some societies do nothing but pray for rain.

Concern to eat nutritious food should be as great as an intention to live a healthy life, but neither of these is as important as the quest for knowledge and wisdom. If, as the elderly so often instruct the young, wisdom comes with age, then the longer we live the wiser we should become. "Does not the ear try words as the palate tastes food? Wisdom is with the aged, and understanding in length of days" (Job 12:11-12). Though food makes no one wise, food makes us live, and life makes us wise. Perhaps only the squirrel who first ate acorns is wise enough to answer whether the acorn or the oak grew first. Or perhaps only the human who first ate squirrels is wise enough. The Edenic tree of knowledge either coincidentally bore apples, or the apple tree accidentally bore knowledge. Either way, the more direct way of getting at the root of knowledge is to eat apples, not animals that eat apples. "Well said," concludes Voltaire's *Candide*. "But we must cultivate our gardens."

While Mary had a little lamb,
and a little beef, and a little ham,
another little girl in Africa,
and a third young child in Asia,
ate next to nothing.

9.

THE PROBLEM OF
BEING A FLESH EATER
(WITH NO IDEA OF THE PROBLEM)

*You ask me why Pythagoras abstained from eating meat.
For my part I wonder what was the disposition, idea,
or motive of the first man who put to his mouth a thing
slaughtered and touched with his lips the flesh of a dead
animal.... Actually, the reasons why those primitive
people first started the eating of flesh was probably their
utter poverty.*

PLUTARCH
"The Eating of Meat"

A SKED WHY HE DID not eat meat, George Bernard Shaw
answered that that is putting the cart before the horse
and in turn asked: "Why *do* you eat meat?" But the one with
whom he spoke remained silent. What carnivore can list as
many reasons for the necessity of flesh eating as we have done
for its superfluity? What philosopher has written a convincing
tract for the cause of carnivorism? What poet has lamented
the misunderstood lives of the butcher and the executioner?
What prophet has bewailed his people's worship of the golden
carrot? So, how does it come to pass that carnivorism is such
an omnipresent part of the Western and, particularly, the

American diet? We, with Plutarch, must ask, "Just why do people eat meat?"

The three mainsprings that have perpetuated carnivorism are tradition, imitation, and sensation. Concerning sensation, what tastes good to one person cannot be disputed by another. One man's meat is another man's poison and an other woman's vegetarianism. If flesh tastes good to someone, then what is valid for the carnivore is simply vapid for the vegetarian. Not much more can be said about sensation, so to tradition and imitation we shall devote the balance of this discussion. Tradition: one's parents ate it, so one eats it, and one's children eat it. Imitation: everyone else eats it, so one wants to be the same as everyone else; everyone tells one to eat it, so one does as one is told.

Of all members of the animal kingdom, humanity is the least ruled by instinct: hence its ruling the animal kingdom. Freedom from instinct is at times an advantage and at other times a hindrance. Analogous to potential for change, this freedom makes precarious the wisdom ancestors learned through trial and error, through take and mistake. Thus humans first ate flesh even though they did not have the guts to do it nor even the intestines. If just one generation fails in preserving the proper tradition but instead introduces a detrimental one, the whole of humanity can suffer for thousands of years.

The hand that winds the mainsprings of tradition and imitation is indoctrination. An illiterate, primitive culture communicates orally, while a literate, technological one does so through media, especially print media. (So that's why you've endured here this long!) The long-literate West abounds with much media machinery, so to trace the cause of its heavy carnivorism we need not excavate any archaeological site, but need only read its newspapers and magazines, listen to its radios and podcasts, watch its TV and films, peruse its placards and billboards, and cruise its rest stops on the interstate and websites on the internet. Either we, like everyone else, will become indoctrinated into carnivorism, or we, more like ourselves, will become wary of it and might thereby guard against it. This is not to say that carnivorism was introduced by the television; however, only our American culture makes both eating flesh and watching TV such integral parts of its meals. Both are possible only in an affluent society, whose affluence creates a market for advertisements, whose marketplace aims is to squander our affluence. As yet, no frozen TV dinner is vegan.

The prophet Daniel resolved not to defile himself with the king's rich food and wine, and wished instead to be given vegetables and water. That he proved himself healthier by it is not our point; why we look to his example is his willingness to defy the king. Many are easily affected by the whims of an influential few, while many simply follow where custom directs, horses at the end of a tether hardly inquiring of effects, hardly caring about causes. Those who follow only the well-trodden path, who never think of their incidental means toward their accidental end, who neither act out their thoughts nor think out their actions, can nevertheless be good and kind. Maybe as many as half of all the Mr. Chuck Steaks and Ms. Virginia Hams of our Pepsi generation would refrain from eating flesh if they themselves had to slaughter and butcher Elsie the Cow and Porky the Pig. Asceticism is not the issue here: it is not wrong that something tastes good, or that eating gives pleasure. But it is questionable when one's pleasure must depend on another's pain.

In the early 1970s, a drunken band of Caucasian Brazilian hunters ventured into the Amazon jungle and slaughtered a small tribe of Amerindians. This was no new event, but this particular case was brought to court and to world view. The drunkards were accused of murder but acquitted because the judge held them irresponsible: the band of hunters did not consider the Amerindians to be humans, but animals. Therefore the judge deemed they be tried for killing animals…which was no crime according to the law. Instead they were reprimanded, instructed that Amerindians indeed are humans, and dismissed. If Brazilian justice had been followed, all those on trial at Nuremburg would have been exonerated. Had they first stumbled on a flock of geese or a family of monkeys, the hunters might never have killed the Amerindians. Ernest Hemingway, a notorious hunter, said he killed animals instead of killing himself. (But he still, finally, killed himself.) The confusion of treating humans as animals merely affirms the humanity of animals and the bestiality of humans. During that terrible European era of Nazism, Jews and Poles were often transported to concentration camps in cattle cars. Yet, to this day, cattle are still transported to slaughterhouses in cattle cars. Though it is deplorable that humans were treated as animals, it is also tragic that animals are still treated "as animals." Jewish survivors of the death camps predominantly became vegetarians—because they knew what it was to be treated as animals.

Nine million people were exterminated in concentration camps throughout Europe in one decade; presently, nine million animals are executed in American slaughterhouses in one day, every day. Germans in communities near the camps contended they had no idea what went on inside, or at least they had no proof of it. Similarly, most Americans have no idea of what goes on in slaughterhouses, since their only proof is well concealed in their barbecued Buchenwald burgers and their hot Dachau dogs. Those with some idea of what might be seen nevertheless have never seen it. People cannot be expected to venture out of their way to seek something unpleasant, especially when every device to keep them unaware is employed by those who stand to profit from collective ignorance. How does this occur? A crowded city street is being prepared for widening, and everyone responsible for the road's congestion thinks it a great shame to see that the row of trees along the road is being marked for destruction. Some circulate petitions, or send outraged letters to editors, or march with protest signs: the petitions are written on paper, the letters printed on newspaper, the signs inscribed on cardboard, all from trees. But few feel sorrow for these trees; these trees grew in forests far away from city sight. Few comprehend the connection between a seedling crushed under heel and a scrap of paper tossed into the gutter, between towering pines and the Sunday *New York Times*.

Likewise with flesh and the animal from which it is severed. People say they love animals, but the animals they love are only dogs and cats, not calves and lambs. Perhaps the dichotomy is due simply to duplicity, but people relegate farm animals into a different class from family pets. This distinction rests neither upon human intelligence, nor upon human contention of the animals' supposed lack of it. Inconsistency carried to the extreme of incoherency is the only excuse for feeling disgusted about the eating of horse flesh but not by the eating of cow flesh. Do caretakers who feed pork to their pets know that the hog is more intelligent than any cat or dog?

Suppose we return a few years later to that widened road, now a superhighway. Every morning heaps of smashed bodies on its pavement act as immobile answers to the eternal question "Why did the chicken cross the road?" Having not gotten to the other side of the road, but rather the other side of life, they are removed by highway maintenance crews well before morning rush hour traffic. But animals throughout the day make the road their dead end. Passing motorists confronted with the carnage sincerely feel pity, even at 100 km/h, as they return home to conduct animal experiments in their kitchens and then to consume carcasses killed by no accident. Where is the logic, and where the justice?

People hardly ponder over pigs when they eat a pork chop, or over cows when they eat a hamburger, or upon the slaughterhouse when they eat a porterhouse. Maintaining this cover-up are the many crews employed by the flesh industries, which tidy every roadway between the slaughterhouse and the marketplace. These roads are everywhere; we all live on one. As the road to Hell is often said to be paved with good intentions, a Holocaust scholar once wrote that the road to Auschwitz was paved with indifference. We could judge both indifference and ignorance as irremissible, and attempt to publicize the otherwise obscured atrocities. Forbidden to bring an audience into the abattoir, we can bring an abattoir to the audience. Probably the first such film is Georges Franju's *Blood of the Beasts*, a short documentary depicting a Parisian abattoir. Filmed during a single day in 1949, it first depicts early morning cityscapes, then an amorous couple embracing and several schoolchildren playing, and then contrasts those adjoining outdoor scenes with those indoors: a horse, a cow, a calf, and several sheep, all being slaughtered by human hands and transported upon human shoulders, before mass mechanization. A scant twenty-two minutes long, it is posted in three segments on YouTube, which limits air time to ten minutes. Pirated and first uploaded in December 2007, by July 2009 its first segment had been viewed 21,000 times, its second segment 15,000 times, and its third and shortest and most gruesome segment only 6,000 times. The rate of attrition is edifying. The film short sometimes is shown in college film programs before the featured full-length film, so few filmgoers flee. Its sensitive audiences of aesthetes are of course horrified. Yet few see the connection between what they view and what they chew: after the feature film, the students sleepwalk to the same campus hangout as last week to snack on the same burgers as last week, seasoned with much catsup but no compunction.

In the case of human abuse of animals, when the facts are presented, people react with disbelief, disaffection, indifference...or vegetarianism. The facts have been disclosed in various vegetarian and humanitarian polemics, but carnivorism somehow persists. Galileo's contemporaries shunned peering through his telescope not because they feared seeing Jupiter's moons, but because the sight would have shaken their illusion of geocentricism. More is at stake than the carnivores' comfort should they visit a slaughterhouse; their whole diet might subsequently change, and that is a larger part of daily habit than most are willing to modify. Few eaters of flesh want to know that animals live and die painfully, or that they die at all; in fact few seem to know animals even live. Knowing everything about braising beef, few know anything about raising cattle.

Patron ignorance is further enforced by the location of slaughterhouses in isolated rural areas. The major exception is Chicago, once the "hog butcher of the world," now mostly for Illinois. Flesh merchants can ship live cows across state lines unmonitored, but dead ones must pass federal inspection. Thus Armour has redistributed its forces to dozens of smaller armories across the country so that it must meet only the usually less stringent state laws. Wheat, spilled from the feed cars, now grows along the derelict railroad tracks. The bone yard has been bulldozed over. Most of the buildings, where many millions of animals fell victims to slaughter crews, now have fallen victims to wrecking crews. A handful of large flesh refinery factories still operate among the few remaining abandoned slaughterhouses, but otherwise the notorious Union Stockyard is now mostly an industrial park. Presently, the only visible testament to the site of Upton Sinclair's book *The Jungle* is the entrance gate, designated an historic landmark—by Mayor Daley of 1968 police riot notoriety.

The gate very closely resembles that of another historic site: Dachau, now a mausoleum museum. The buildings, the barbed wire, the ovens where hundreds of Hansels were burned, the showers where thousands of Gretels were gassed, all are reconstructions. In a yard where people were shot in target practice, flowers now flourish: as any modern farmer knows, blood provides excellent fertilizer. Just as flesh for city markets comes mostly from slaughterhouses in rural areas, though its inmates worked in many factories of nearby Munich the concentration camp was located near only the small community of Dachau. Dead bodies are best buried in basements, where few go and where the light is dim. Visitors need not be Jewish to sense the doom looming in the Dachau air even to this day. But why is it only some people sense that same doom today at the Union Stockyards? Easterners would attribute this to blocked chakras, Westerners to congested nasal passages. Yet no matter from what direction we look, the greatest block is in our field of vision. What the merchants of venison conceal through obfuscation is one thing; what they choose to reveal through advertisement is quite another. Many consumers still believe animals are raised in arboreal dells of bucolic tranquility, where the sheep are tenderly herded by Timmy and Lassie, where the chickens scamper playfully outside the front porch and peck at Gramps' feet, and where the cows are lovingly milked by Mom.

The news media and their advertisers to which they are beholden reinforce the erroneous education of the orectic consumer. Scholars, poets, philosophers, and philanthropists have long recognized vegetarianism as humanity's humane way of life, but cattle barons and worshippers of golden calves under golden arches have cloaked with cloak and dagger the carnage of carnivorism. Since 1985, one dollar from the sale of every cow and steer is diverted by American federal government mandate to the National Cattlemen's Beef Board. Thus the purchase of every Big Mac or Double Whopper contributes to their coffers to camouflage their coffins. "Beef: It's What's for Dinner," commands the Beef Board. Similarly, the National Pork Producers Board receives 45 cents for every $100 in hog sales. "Pork: the Other White Meat," proclaims the Pork Board. "Got milk?" asks the National Milk Producers Board. While Wendy no longer asks, "Where's the beef?" dare she ask, "Where's the wealth? And where's the health?" Their wealth trumps our health, as few comparable industry-funded councils and boards exist to propagandize for carrots and peas, or for peanut butter and jelly.

The West has become a herd of sheep led by blind and blinding shepherds, a race of people hardly different from the herds they eat. Old shepherds led by staff and dog, new ones by advertising and indoctrination. "Woe to the shepherds who destroy and scatter the sheep of my pasture, says the Lord" (Jeremiah 23:1). To cite just a few 20th century examples, in Soviet gulags such as Karaganda, Nazi concentration camps such as Dachau, Pol Pot Cambodia, and Bosnian Serb Srebrenica, civilians were first held captive and then slaughtered by barbarian armies whose weapons of incarceration were barbed wire and machine guns. Now society's tools of indoctrination are its news media, through which humans are robbed of their health while animals are robbed of their lives. Perhaps the exploited animals' own hormones as well as the chemical hormones injected into their flesh affect the humans eating that hormone-rich flesh, for instance in turn to become exploited, so that carnivores will believe they must exploit animals. Yet, here is where humans do differ from animals. It is a mystery how factory-farmed animals tolerate their misery; whereas under the same circumstances, humans often resort to suicide or willed starvation.

Our difference from animals is most marked in our uniquely human ability to despise ourselves. If one must first love oneself to love others, then perhaps also one first must despise oneself to despise others. No wonder the American government, through the gauntleted hand of the USDA, actively promotes carnivorism. All governments seek both aggressive and submissive soldiers: aggressive so that they will defeat their enemies, submissive so that they will allow their own servitude in the military. A soldier is no less exploited than a lamb or a hog or a cow; the difference is that the beef cow is slaughtered after two years, whereas the soldier, if he survives combat, is discharged and set free.

We have already seen in chapter 6 how flesh eaters assimilate the traits either of other fierce flesh-eating animals or of the docile farm animals whose flesh they eat. Tartars, famous for ferocity and for feeding on excessive amounts of flesh, illustrate the first case. Yet those who desire to be as fierce as Tartars, who wish to be conquerors rather than conquered, merely reflect exploitation by the state, and illustrate the second case. Although Tartars charging on the backs of horses would easily overpower Buddhists meditating beneath bodhi trees, to whom would we attribute the greater wisdom? When not depicted meditating, the Buddha is shown laughing. The meek shall inherit the mirth.

The harbinger humans who first killed each other with clubs learned the trick and perfected the technique from killing quarry. The opening sequence of the film *2001* illustrates this precisely. Humanity become warriors only after becoming carnivores; thus world peace is attainable only after we all again become vegetarians. Now, announcing that flesh eating induces aggression is not the point here, nor should it be anywhere. Quite the contrary, it is best kept quiet, because some people would devour flesh with that very goal in mind, that is, if they have a mind. In the late 1800s, an evangelist roamed frontier America preaching against the evils of eating flesh, attributing its practice to excitation of the passions. Everywhere he proselytized, its consumption increased.

The majority of humanity quietly and inconspicuously tends to its personal affairs, unmoved either by pleas for benevolence or by provocations for violence. Sometimes, however, we will be stirred. All sorts of boycotts of food and consumer products attest to this. If the plight of a nearly extinct species arouses public sentiment, then the next step is recognition that each individual animal regardless of its species is a being as distinct as the species itself. The news media coverage of and activists commotion over the perennial baby seal slaughters in Norway and Canada demonstrate such concern for individuals whose species is not so near extinction. For reasons unknown, schools of dolphins follow schools of tuna, the dolphins swimming near the surface of the water, the tuna below. Tuna fishers in trawlers track dolphins to locate schools of tuna and, for many years until newer nets and upgraded technologies were developed, they captured and killed both, but ostensibly canned only the tuna, although DNA tests years later confirmed that they sometimes canned both. On these terms, many people, outraged about killing dolphins, refused to eat tuna; their next step is to foment outrage about killing tuna, and to refuse to eat tuna. In 1976, a conflict at sea arose between England and Iceland concerning fishing rights. Let us set aside such concerns for the rights of England, or the rights of Iceland; let us consider the rights of fish.

Still, Englishmen and Icelanders, fishermen and canners, eaters of dolphins and of tunas, have rights. No hate should be felt for carnivorous humans any more than against carnivorous animals. We should not compel a human not to kill an animal. We cannot prohibit murder of animals nor, were there such laws, could we form a gendarmerie to enforce them. Yet the cry against the false bliss of ignorance and the death kiss of insouciance should never cease. To this purpose the individual must be the watchdog, but need never bite; loud barks usually suffice to destroy institutionalized ignorance, which quickly flees our lanterns and flashlights like a black cat in the night.

Our struggle is as much to disseminate information as to educate against misinformation. Consider the long misunderstood short life of the veal calf. Veal is white not because the calf is milk-fed, as the veal industry would lead us to believe; rather, it is because in the veal crate the calf is bred anemic, immobile, and in the dark, and because at the slaughterhouse its blood is eviscerated fully. Since half of all calves are males who cannot gain admittance into the land of milk and money, without a veal industry to subsidize the milk industry, milk would be twice the price. Farm families, who make their living from milking their cows dry, know the true price that must be paid; thus many do not eat veal. They abstain from what they know, but embrace what they do not know, since they do eat other sorts of flesh. In these matters, the typical carnivore generally knows nothing...and eats everything.

Through news media, the flesh industries encourage narcose sensibilities in their audiences by humanizing the consumed so as not to dehumanize the consumers. Hence, since 1961 and 50 years and 80 ads later, sorrowful Charlie the Tuna repeatedly fails at his attempts to get canned and, just the opposite, marching little children sing of wishing they were Oscar Mayer wieners "because then everyone would be in love with me." But one clever child marches to a different drummer and sings he is glad he is not a wiener "for there would be nothing left of me." Transforming eaten animals into people, and making people wish they were eaten animals, merely signifies an underlying condition of carnivorism: its substitute for cannibalism. Some vegetarian wannabes describe themselves as being *almost vegetarian*, which actually is little different from being *almost cannibal*. A brand name for a Virginia Ham is "Hansel and Gretel." It is well known what the witch wished to do with them. But not so well known is the real reason they were lost in the forest. For this we must consult Grimms' fairy tale, not the Humperdinck opera. It occurs that their cruel mother had not enough to feed her whole family, and so sent them away into the woods to starve to death so she and her husband would have enough to eat for themselves. Obviously the witch suffered from the same famine and wished to vanquish her hunger in her own solitary fashion. This tale parallels the way dairy farmers deal with veal.

Our sad human saga might very well reach its end in an oven such as the one intended for Hansel but which instead swallowed up the witch. Quite distinct from the oven is the garden. Our biblical history began with Adam and Eve, first with their creation, then with their transgression. The links from Adam and Eve to Hansel and Gretel are Cain and Abel. When Cain (a tiller of the ground) saw Abel (a keeper of sheep) sacrifice an animal, he assumed killing was good. It is well known what Cain did to Abel. But it was Abel, not Cain, who was the first killer. Hence the first killer human became the first human killed. Whether humans will ever cease killing other humans depends on whether humans will ever cease killing animals, and that depends on whether humans will ever cease eating animals. After a year, few newly minted vegetarians again desire flesh; such a desire is an impure thought brought forth by impure food, in this case the flesh itself. As long as it is constantly fed, an unhealthy appetite is hardly ever satiated. After a late night steak dinner, the engorged gourmand wakes in the morning with an unsatisfied appetite for still more gore, this time for a breakfast of bacon and eggs. Desires, especially those for which no moderation is exercised, easily become vices. Oscar Wilde advised that the best way to overcome a vice is to succumb to it; perhaps this proved effective for Wilde, but too many others squander their entire lives succumbing.

For many, flesh eating is a pleasure. But it is the pleasure of Dionysius whose swords of Damocles hang over dining room chairs by the hairs of the very animals whose flesh is eaten. Are there not greater pleasures at less risk? If truly carnivorous, humans would delight more in the gore of raw flesh than in the fragrance of ripe fruit, and would feel more at peace in an abattoir than in an orchard. Quite the contrary, only disguise and disinfectant make flesh palatable. It is dressed in nearly everything except clothing, and is salted and peppered, sugared and simmered, spiced and diced, MSG'ed and BHT'ed, toasted and roasted, filleted and fried, foiled and broiled, pickled and poached, poked and smoked, barbecued and stewed, in short eaten every way but fresh and raw and whole, so that those who devour it might feel "civilized." Even when raw, flesh is preserved with sodium nitrites, which conceal the gangrenous sight of putrefaction. Delegating the slaughter to someone else, and consuming the animal only after it has been several days dead, human carnivores ally themselves not with the animal kingdom's predators, but with its scavengers.

Since carnivores neither see nor go near a slaughterhouse, nor wish to, what do they see? Only the fast food franchise and supermarket facades of glass and Formica and stainless steel. The flesh industry is all too aware of what its consumers want to eat and want not to see regarding what they eat. Those rare shoppers who request observation of cutting rooms are politely refused entry; managers provide excuses or apologies, saying liability insurance does not cover visitors, or citing company policy. "It is for your own protection," one manager instructed a curious customer, meaning safety and sanitation, but implying innocence and ignorance.

A masquerade even lurks within the lexicon: the disingenuous definition of *flesh* as *meat* is but the beginning of society's many self-aggrandizing fictions. According to what cryptogram does *flesh* become *meat*? Picture a burger in a bun and topped with lettuce and relish: to the average carnivore, that is nothing offensive. Picture just the naked hamburger patty without the bun: that is nothing offensive. Picture the chopped meat uncooked and unshaped: again, nothing offensive. Picture the chopped meat packaged on a cardboard tray and in cellophane wrap on the supermarket shelf: again again, nothing offensive. Picture the slab of meat still a chunk awaiting grinding: still nothing offensive. Imagine (for this next stage, you likely never before saw this, so will stop *picturing* and begin *imagining*) the chunk not yet carved from the carcass, hanging from a meat hook: here might be something disquieting, here you might avert your gaze from the split and stripped body of something half recognizable as a cow, or recognizable as half a cow. Imagine the dead body of Elsie the Cow shackled by one hind leg, hanging upside down, awaiting evisceration and skinning: here indeed is much to lose repose over, maybe even lose your lunch over; you hardly wish to see large dead animals; small fry and fish and chickens are enough. Imagine Elsie at the eternal moment of death, throat cut by a cutthroat, hind leg broken at the shackle, and thrust upside down: this you likely wish to avoid imagining, and certainly wish to avoid seeing. Imagine Elsie alive and relatively well, shuffling around her crowded pen in the feedlot: once again, here is nothing offensive, this does not affront your sensibilities.

Consumers remain almost totally ignorant of the moribund methods undertaken by animal undertakers to deliver flesh into the picnic casket. Consumers do not wish to be reminded of the lives of the animals whose flesh they eat, so producers do not remind them. Our materialistic society consists of but two classes of citizens: not aristocracy and plebians, not masters and slaves, not quite military and civilians, not even politicians and electorate, and certainly not scholars and students, but rather producers and consumers. In order for producers and consumers to conduct "business as usual" without hindrance from their consciences or from our criticisms, the two classes form a secret, silent partnership. Producers pretend to tell the truth, and consumers pretend to believe them.

Meatpackers do not just hide behind facades, they also fabricate falsehoods. Let's look specifically at chickens. Just as modern slaughterhouses are large factories whose disassembly lines take only minutes to tear chicken bodies apart, modern farms are huge factories whose assembly lines take only weeks to piece those bodies together. Depictions of de-beaked hens cramped their entire short lives like sardines in a can would hardly sell the "tender chickens" of Perdue Farms. Packaging shapes products to suit consumer desires, and advertising shapes consumer desires to fit the products. Perdue Farms paints its products not just with ridiculous whitewash, but also with mendacious hogwash. Until he retired from personally hawking his chickens in 1994, Frank Perdue assured us that his chickens lived in a house "that's just chicken heaven." And he assured us this in all imaginable media, even underground on dimly lit posters on cavernous walls inside New York City subway stations bordering on human hell. So long as their doomed animals fatten, factory farmers present this as living proof that the well fed are also the well bred. If you were condemned to death row, and confined to your tiny prison cell, which contained only a cot and table and a toilet, and administered growth hormones, and allowed only to eat and sleep and eat, you, too, would fatten.

What industry can be trusted to treat humanely their corporal livestock in bondage when they clearly care more for their corporate stocks and bonds? And what government can be respected whose existing animal welfare laws exclude farm animals? Those few laws concerning farm animals address mostly how they are to die, not how they are to live, and anyway are outdated and seldom enforced. Such laws at least look good on paper. Meanwhile, our primary access to information in print form is that disseminated by the United States Department of Agriculture (USDA) and its subsidiary National Agricultural Statistics Service (NASS). The USDA publishes scholarly research articles, factual instructions manuals, and public relations boondoggles. A few of its publications, for instance its *Yearbook of Agriculture*, shuffle together all three. These thick hardbound annuals sometimes total 900 pages. Published for a hundred years, from 1894 to 1992, its intended audience slowly shifted from producers to consumers, in other words, to us. In celebration of the USDA's own hundredth anniversary of its reign, the editor of the 1962 volume wrote in his preface that the yearbooks are now becoming "a sampler of progress...addressed more to non-farmers than to farmers."

Let's examine the *Yearbook of Agriculture* for 1975, the threshold year of first publication of Peter Singer's seminal *Animal Liberation*. Subtitled *That We May Eat*, we are the *We*, and its language reveals official USDA dogma that animals are servitors of the human race, machines that function to convert plant food to flesh food. Page 123 states: "They [cattle] will convert crop residues...into beef and milk for human consumption." Page 125 admits: "Only three decades ago Americans depended on countless backyard flocks to provide them with chicken for the table. Today, however, broiler production is industrialized in much the same way as the production of cars, shoes, or TV sets." Page 133 tells us: "The hog is a rapid, prolific, and relatively efficient meat-making machine." And then we are fed outright lies on page 126: "Today's broiler [hen]...is fed better, housed and cared for better, and pampered in many ways." Incarceration and over-crowding of chickens is described on page 132 as "...intimate contact with his peers." A generation later, now even carni-vores acknowledge that the USDA was awash in hogwash.

Thoughts, and the words that express those thoughts, extend far and wide, capture attention, hold imagination, mold lives, and command action. (You obviously agree, else instead of reading, you might have gone fishing.) The English language has loaded its crafts of communication with many disguises. What is called *fleisch* for both animals and humans in German, is differentiated as either *meat* or *flesh* in English. Animals have *hides*, but humans possess *skin*. Animals are *slaughtered*, but humans are *murdered*. In war, the human enemy is reduced to the status of inanimate objects, lower than even animals. For example, an American general discuss-ing nuclear strike capabilities never once implied killing, but instead spoke of "blast parameters" and "fallout interfaces."

Society's most strictly tabooed subjects are those that reveal the negative side of life, and for the West the most odi-ous aspect of life is death. It is buried under two meters of fertile soil, or inside two pages of fine print. Thus, flesh adver-tisements intentionally camouflage and obfuscate. Our ideal-ized views of ourselves are reflected through the mirror of our media; those mirrors that reflect images we do not wish to see, we cover or remove from view. If a book, we simply close it.

The American Meat Institute (AMI) is our nation's oldest and largest and most influential of all organ organizations. The AMI is quick to uphold the death taboo, as we clearly see in its advertisements. One ad campaign was released between 1950 and 1954, the post-war boom years, after a war marked by meat rationing among civilians. Among other periodicals, those ads ran in monthly installments in two leading literary and social commentary periodicals, *Harper's Magazine* and *The Atlantic*. The series presents a seemingly facetious facade of smiling animals, even when on their way to market. Paradoxically, animals are also portrayed as adversaries that require "costly feeds." Animals are not raised, rather "meat is grown." Meatpackers deal "in buying livestock and selling it as meat," while animals are merely a "storehouse of meat, on the hoof" converted for the consumer "into steaks and roasts for his home freezer." So, "next time you eye a meat animal, look at the eatin' parts." After all, "you want just ham—not a whole hog." To aid this, the cattleman takes the cattle from pasture and imprisons them in feedlots where they are grain-fed: "He takes them to his beef factory and feeds them—fills out their frames," giving them "the kind of living that his boarders enjoy." But until what point? Alas, the destiny of pigs is more descriptive: "They spend the summer and early fall growing to pork-chop size." "Summertime is always the time when a new meat crop is growing up." And then in the fall, "Pigs come into a packing plant in one piece; they leave in as many as eighty different pork products." That is seventy-nine pieces too many.

But enough. Is it such a big step from looking at an animal and seeing only dead meat and money, to viewing a human and thinking only of coerced sex and servitude? Evidence does show that boys who abuse their pets often grow up to become husbands who abuse their wives. The day will dawn when future generations will view carnivorism with the same disdain and disbelief as our present generation views slavery and Nazism. Meanwhile, in our consumer society where ads and logos assault our senses, vegetarians every day get shoved down their throats an onslaught of flesh: Big Mac and Burger King; KFC and BLT; bacon and eggs for breakfast, franks and beans for lunch, meat and potatoes for supper. Eat, eat, eat. Buy, buy, buy. Kill, kill, kill. Caviar without caveat. We might close our eyes, yet the odors of crematoria still fill our nostrils in the workplace lunchroom. Carnivores cannot understand that smells that whet their appetites instead for vegetarians ruin ours. Most Americans' surviving contacts with farm animals are initiated with a knife and concluded with a napkin, and preceded by something smelling good to them coming from the kitchen and followed by something smelling bad to others coming from the bathroom.

The USDA's NASS keeps careful tabs on those gustatory and olfactory transactions, so let's get it straight from the horse's mouth. *Agricultural Statistics 2008*, published in 2008, provides the numbing numbers for 2006, when the American population reached its milestone and millstone 300 million (Table 13-1). During that single year, the average American ate 110 pounds of beef cows, 63 pounds of veal calves, 46 pounds of pigs, 61 pounds of broiler chickens, 13 pounds of turkeys, 32 pounds of chicken eggs, and 17 pounds of fishes (Table 13-7). Also in 2006, this already stuffed average American made room to drink 208 pounds of milk (Table 8-21), and to eat five pounds of butter, 32 pounds of cheese, and 15 pounds of ice cream (Table 8-30). Let's stop and take a break, even if only to make room for dessert, though surely not ice cream.

That's 342 pounds, almost a single Shylock pound of flesh per day; plus 208 pounds of milk, and 52 pounds of milk

products. We don't know precisely for whose *capita* these
per capita averages account, for a behemoth macho male or a
petite svelte female; nor whether the general population from
which these data are extrapolated, and from which this head
is decapitated, includes resolute vegetarians who eat none of
the above animals, or absolute vegans who eat none of the
above, or destitute carnivores who eat flesh only out of cans
of dog and cat food. Furthermore, measurements in pounds
rather than in portions do not enable us to fully grasp the
enormity of these quantities. Even more revealing would be
measurements in numbers of animals eaten by an average carnivore; flesh is eaten one portion at a time, but animals are
killed one life at a time.

The NASS never has calculated animal lives per human life,
in part because far less than half of an animal's body is actually eaten; nor would it want to calculate this figure, else some
vegetarian zealots yell the death toll from the rafters, or blab
it all over the internet, or commission skywriting airplanes to
inscribe it in the heavens above Manhattan or Los Angeles or
Chicago, and tag it with the voice of authority "according to
the USDA." Thus such tallow tallies bandied about in tracts
of vegetarian propaganda, including this one, are conjectural
and apocryphal, much like the eight glasses of water we're told
to drink daily, for which no one can cite any study or source.
But wait; the NASS does provide a tally of animals marching
in funeral processions to federally inspected slaughterhouses;
just remember, this disregards the billions of fish, sea animals,
and wild animals who die outside of USDA jurisdiction, and
the millions of farm animals who never leave the farm alive.

The numbing numbers for 2006 are: 33.7 million cattle
and cows, and 748,000 calves (Table 7-12); 104.8 million hogs

(Table 7-29); 2.8 million sheep (Table 7-51); 562,000 goats (Table 7-80); 102,000 horses (Table 7-80); 9 *billion* chickens, 255,000 turkeys, and 28,000 ducks (Table 8-50). Though they detour the abattoir, scramble into this 91.3 *billion* eggs (Table 8-62). Because humans generally eat the entire egg except for its shell, an annual per capita total for eggs is indeed provided, namely 256 eggs (Table 8-58). In other words, every three days Americans perform two abortions on chickens in their kitchens.

When Chicago opened its Union Stockyards in 1865, America ended its War between the States, and embarked in earnest on its War between the Species. Calculation of the millions of animals killed within those Stockyards during its hundred-year history would conjure a number so huge that the real horror would remain incomprehensible. Who can fathom what is even a million? We should ponder a smaller figure: only the hogs killed in one single record-breaking day in 1924: 123,000. Probably we could count that many hogs in one day and one night. Surely we would not fall asleep, as though we were counting sheep.

AN APOLOGETIC ADDENDUM
SOME SECOND, AND SECONDARY, THOUGHTS

> *For the great majority of people a kind of training every-*
> *where takes the place of culture. It is achieved by exam-*
> *ple, by custom and the very early and firm impression of*
> *certain concepts, before any experience, understanding,*
> *and power of judgment existed to disturb the work. Thus*
> *ideas are implanted which afterwards cling so firmly and*
> *are not to be shaken by any instruction just as if they were*
> *innate, and they have often been regarded as such, even*
> *by philosophers. In this way we can with equal effort*
> *impress people with what is right and rational, or with*
> *what is most absurd. For example...we can accustom*
> *them to renounce all animal food, as in Hindustan, or to*
> *devour the still warm and quivering pieces cut out from*
> *the living animal, as in Abyssinia; to eat human beings as*
> *in New Zealand, or to sacrifice their children to Moloch,*
> *to castrate themselves, to fling themselves voluntarily on*
> *the funeral pile of the deceased—in a word, to do any-*
> *thing we wish.*
>
> ARTHUR SCHOPENHAUER
> *The World as Will and Representation,*
> Vol. II, Chapter VI, "On the Doctrine
> of Abstract Knowledge, or Knowledge of Reason"

MUSLIMS AND JEWS are forbidden to eat pigs, cam-
els, toads, scorpions, and centipedes. The pig taboo
is shared also by Jakuts of Siberia, Sami of Finland, and

Malagasy of Madagascar. Chickens are forbidden food to Mongols; cows to Hindus and Parsis of India; rabbits to Chinese; eggs to Ganda of Uganda and Caribbees of the Caribbean; milk to Dayaks of Borneo, Malayas of Malaysia, Dravidians of India, and Ashanti of Ghana; fish to Zulus of South Africa; humans to all humans, at least in theory if not in practice; and all the above are forbidden foods to all strict vegetarians. Ancient Greeks, Romans, and Aztecs ate dogs; but if they merely attempt to do so, modern Americans are charged with cruelty to animals.

Sanctions against one kind of flesh food exist only for consumers of other kinds. Anti-cannibalistic instincts apply only to carnivores and are strongest in those who are the strongest carnivores. Carnivores generally do not eat other carnivores: if a lion could eat a tiger, a lion could eat a lion. Cultures that ate dogs were only sporadic carnivores, and their dogs ate even less flesh than they did dogs. Just as carnivorous humans never grew claws and fangs, and instead utilized knives and spears, neither did they develop instincts to prohibit use of those weapons against other humans. Instead they enacted laws easily ignored, barely enforced, and frequently forgotten. "No matter how many laws they passed increasing the severity of the punishments inflicted on those who ate meat in secret," wrote Samuel Butler in *Erewhon*, "the people found means of setting them aside as fast as they were made."

In 1857 in India, a new British rifle was introduced whose cartridges had to be bitten open before loading. Rumors circulated among the ranks of the Hindu and Muslim sepoys that the lubricant coating the cartridges was either tallow from cow fat or lard from pig fat. To a Hindu, licking the flesh of the sacred cow is an unpardonable sin; to a Muslim, tasting the flesh of the desecrated pig is an insufferable pollution. Because of deep social injustice, the Sepoy Rebellion against the British was inevitable, but the mutiny was incited by the coating on the cartridges.

During the sixth century BCE in India, Hindu priests sacrificed more and more cattle. The drain on the congregants' source of milk and labor became so burdensome that a heretic protested against this and other religious impositions. About the same age as Christ when he began his ministry, this leader preached for an end to animal slaughter of all kinds. His campaign was so successful that a whole new religion evolved from him. A half a millennium later, around the time of the birth of Christ, even the Hindu priests ceased sacrifices. The name of that rebellious prophet was Buddha.

Buddha was awake amid a nation of somnambulists, so he could rightfully preach. But *my* right is rather dubious. I only guess at the difference between truth and falsehood; I hardly know right from wrong; I see the distinction between only some good but not all evil; I know little about love and less than that about hate; but I do clearly perceive the faint nuances between the important and the unimportant. For instance, I do know that whether one is wise or otherwise, it is important to weigh the differences between truth and falsehood, right and wrong, good and evil, and love and hate. And I do know that if I profess to love animals, then it is right and good and important that I not kill them, though I barely perceive the difference between life and death.

Perhaps my condemnatory rhetoric can give the impression that I hate humans who eat animals, since I love animals. But I do not hate animals that eat animals, and besides, humans are animals, too. The portions of this discourse directed against carnivores were intended as incentive, not insult. Until age 15, I, too, was a carnivore. Some of my best friends and former lovers have been carnivores, that is, until I inspired them to change their lives. The butcher is every bit as worthy a human as the baker (who bakes with lard) and the candlestick-maker (who makes candles with tallow).

The deer and the rabbits around my home do not flee me; the chickadees seeking sunflower seeds perch upon me; my squirrel neighbors and my human neighbors' dogs all have befriended me. And while I interact with a dog as a squirrel up a tree looks on, I hope the squirrel holds no grudge against me. Likewise with humans: when I circulated leaflets in front of their stores, I hoped the butcher and the furrier held no grudge against me. My vehement if not venomous voice sometimes has made me an enemy of strangers, and a stranger to friends. Had I never been moved to action, no one would have mistaken my devotion to one cause as contempt for its opposites. Hate and murder are evils, but what about hate of murder?

Despite all the evil in the world, I have met few evil people. But I do know many unhappy people. Ethical philosophies have equated virtue with happiness; more modern ones equate virtue as a means to happiness. Old or new, is vegetarianism virtuous? It probably is not evil. If virtue comprises happiness and if vegetarianism is virtuous, then vegetarianism engenders happiness. And is vegetarianism healthful? It certainly is not carcinogenic. If health comprises happiness and if vegetarianism is a means to health, then vegetarianism is a means to happiness. Whether in the cause of the humane or the human, whether we do not eat flesh because we do not kill, or we do not kill because we do not eat flesh, the effects are identical.

To the moralist, vegetarianism *is* virtuous; to the nutritionist, vegetarianism *is* healthful.

It is no coincidence that what is harmful to the animal killed and grilled is also unhealthy to the killer and griller. Were it opposite, vegetarianism would garner little interest, this whole discussion would amount to empty erudition, and you would not be reading this. No doubt would have arisen to allay, no heresy would have evolved to foment. But this is not the case. Vegetarianism is both a physical relief and a metaphysical reward. Yet we count among us exceptions those who care about animals but not about themselves (as though they were not animals), those who, as Seneca said, kill themselves with their teeth. These are the self-righteous animal rightists who proclaim their convictions with pins on their lapels, but betray their cause by the livid look on their faces. They do not drink blood, but do drink coffee, Coke, and Coors. (And is it any less revolting to eat soybeans made to taste like flesh than it would be ridiculous to eat flesh made to taste like soybeans?) First we must foster our own well-being, and proceed from there. Then there are those who do foster their well-being, but proceed nowhere. They are the health foods fetishists who care everything about themselves, but nothing about the animals. Let no one make the mistake through their examples that vegetarianism is a philosophy only of the gut.

Our Western vegetarianism provides but one small step toward a more encompassing Eastern ideal: *ahimsa*, complete harmlessness. Upon this ideal alone, I have not hesitated to pronounce *ex cathedra* judgments upon Western society and have rejected the sacred texts of Western religion. Yet I have no intent of fostering Judaic, Christian, or Islamic apostasy solely due to vegetarian tenets. Because who am I to judge? Because who am I?

I use no cosmetics or pharmaceuticals made from or tested on animals, because I use no cosmetics or pharmaceuticals, period. Unless a fanatical member of the National Rifle Association shoots me in the back or a hired assassin of the American Meat Institute slits my throat, I anticipate living in good health to age 90 or 91; but then, when I reach 92, and a physician beseeches me to take some pharmaceutical drug else I die in misery, I cannot now attest to what I will do.

I never broke a bone in my body, despite many calamitous close calls, until on my 39th birthday. Sober but celebratory, I attempted a daredevil dive into a river, and the devil outdid my dare. I shattered a vertebrae, which injured my spinal cord, which left me paraplegic. I was paralyzed, not forever, just the rest of my life; and not everywhere, just below the waist. Nine months later, I experienced enough recovery to begin to walk with leg braces and crutches. Nineteen years later, I continue walking with crutches, including climbing twenty flights of stairs in one hour, and hiking two miles of mountains in one day. And paraplegia is not just about *walk*; among its four other four-letter words, I regained two more of them. My health and stamina partially contributed to my recovery; and my vegetarian diet partially contributed to my health and stamina. While I relinquish any claim to being the world's healthiest vegetarian, I do lay claim to being the world's healthiest paraplegic.

I wear canvas shoes spring through fall, often no shoes in summer, but usually leather shoes in snow in winter. For many years, I used a used leather wallet, which I found in the gutter. But I must confess that to cushion my leg braces, I prefer to wear thick new socks made of sheep's wool.

I switched from flaxseed-based oil paints to synthetic acrylics so that I could paint with brushes made of synthetic nylon hairs, not of natural bristle, camel, or sable; but photographic film is coated with animal-based gelatin, so anyone would surely shudder who knew the endless rolls of film I used to expose and then simply discarded.

I refuse to patronize circuses or rodeos or agricultural fairs because their techniques of training animals are cruel; but I do visit aquaria and zoos and natural history museums. I am not sure which is worse: stuffing dead animals with cotton, or stuffing live animals into cages. And I harbor a (now not so) secret desire to see a bullfight, just once, to prove to myself what I probably can predict, that the Mexican audience at a bullfight is neither more nor less sadistic than American fans at a boxing match.

I wash with only soaps and shampoos made from vegetable oils, and brush my teeth with baking soda instead of yummy toothpaste made partially from animal bones. Most charcoal filters for drinking water are made wholly from charred animal bones, yet I still eat foods that list "filtered water" as an ingredient.

I avoid harming most insects, including the wasps that every year build their colonies of nests in my car shelter just inches above my head; but I do swat mosquitoes, and did battle the slugs and grubs in my outdoor gardens. Because all my wild animal neighbors helped themselves to the fruits of my labors before I could, I no longer cultivate gardens outdoors; instead, in defense of their crops, faraway farmers kill the slugs and grubs and wild animals for me.

I attempted very slowly to convert into a vegetarian a cat with whom I shared my household for a year, but after much rejected food, I gave up. After all, she was already three years a carnivore, and an American cat at that. Her mother and her grandmother and her great-grandmother were all fed lots of flesh, as opposed to, say, an Italian cat, whose mamma, nonna, and bisnonna were fed mostly pasta. I did succeed in reducing her diet to only one-fifth flesh; thus instead of 9 Lives, I fed her only two.

I once held a job in an art library where one of my responsibilities was selecting new books. Its classification scheme was of an older sort, and books on sports were part of the art collection. I unconditionally refused to requisition any books on hunting or fishing, but knowingly ordered paperbacks on art though bound with glues such as Elmer's made from bones such as Elsie's.

Do I suffer from moral hypochondria, or are my self-inflicted moral wounds real and necessary? Old Master oil paintings are primed with rabbit-skin glue, their tempera paints are made from eggs, and caseins from milk. If *The Slaughtered Ox* were painted on rabbit-skin glue and with sable hair brushes, that is Rembrandt's choice, and not mine. If I blind myself to its beauty, I alone lose.

In a society of the flock and the herd, the rational is also the radical. *Radical vegetarianism* means abstinency, and a certain degree of obstinacy. It is dialectical, but also a little diabolical. Its course could lead to a substitution of axioms for insights, but such risks must be taken. These pages are *obiter dicta*, not divine judgments; alternatives, not ultimatums. I have merely exercised my right to regard as false, or at least as equivocal, those maxims that guide life and death in this society. If I had transformed every sentence into a question, would that have been more honest? I make no claim to know

the absolute truth; my claim that a vegetarian's claim is generally closer to the truth than that of a carnivore's merely proves
the limitations of my experience, not of carnivorism. Many
of the writers quoted from or referred to on these pages were
vegetarians, which only proves the provincial nature of what I
read, not the wisdom of vegetarians.

Convictions are easily renounced, but upheld with difficulty.
And refuting one belief does not necessarily provide proof of its
opposite. Though it might be preferable, it is difficult to ponder
vegetarianism without ever taking into account and therefore
taking to task carnivorism. If boldly outspoken vegetarians
become obnoxious, and if carnivores become offended, the
losses of social acceptance for the former and of shaky compla-
cency for the latter are small costs to exchange for an animal's
only life. Expressing love is not enough; we also must express
opinions. And if we fully express opinions on one side, feelings
just may be hurt on the other. Neither prince nor pals should
infringe upon our principles. Our bodies are our temples: dare
we mind our manners, but not our manors?

Carnivores should be asked to expose themselves to the vegetarian dialectic of diet and ethic for one day, for just one day.
Since vegetarians are forcibly indoctrinated in the opposite
each and every day, that is not much to ask. Some things are
easier done than said; once inner inclination is felt, no more
need be said. But if after that single day carnivores do not feel
inspired to modify their diets, then we have done all we can
do. Waiting on the edge of time, watching for the dawn of that
day, that one day, we need not aim to regain the whole of the
Garden of Eden: the Tree of Life is enough. That tree, men-
tioned in only the first and last books of the Bible, is the symbol both of time's beginning and eternity's end. Meanwhile,

until that day, what can we do? Catholics and Muslims and Jews, Blacks and Latinos and Amerindians, gays and grays and girls and women, all in their time have demanded their rights as Americans, and all have been granted or are on their way to being granted them. But no group of animals is able to petition Congress to protect their rights as animals. Both their petition and protection rest with you and me. According to Kant's moral postulate: "You can because you ought."

Though neither an Amos nor a Hosea, a Jeremiah nor an Isaiah, I sense others' revulsion and my own against injustices embedded in our society, and as much for them as for myself I have spoken. Let no one accuse me of acquiescence and self-glossotomy. Let not Isaiah say of me:

> Like a lamb that is led to the slaughter
> and like a sheep that before its shearers is dumb,
> so he opened not his mouth.

Thus this had to be written: not as a voice of sanity amid so much madness—for the distinction is moot and easy to refute—but as a voice of the living amid the silence of the dead.

Posthumous Postscript

EDGAR KUPFER, BORN IN 1906 in Koberwitz near Breslau, was a pacifist. Imprisoned in Dachau, he was blessed either by the gods or by the guards with a clerical job in the concentration camp storeroom. On stolen scraps of paper and with pieces of pencil, he stealthily scribbled a secret diary. For three years he buried his writings, an idea no doubt inspired from burying the dead. On April 29, 1945, Dachau was liberated; Edgar Kupfer was freed.

The *Dachau Diaries,* too, were freed, and published in 1956. By this time Kupfer-Koberwitz had emigrated to Chicago, where he lived a St. Stephen's stone's throw from the Union Stockyards. Based on his Dachau notes kept prior to and shortly after the liberation, he wrote an essay on vegetarianism, which he subsequently translated into his immigrant's English. A carbon copy of the original 38-page typescript from which the following pages are excerpted, along with the four boxes containing the original *Dachau Diaries,* are now preserved in the Special Collection of the Library of the University of Chicago, ironically the same university that formerly housed the Research Laboratories of the American Meat Institute.

In 1979, while literally thumbing through the University of Chicago's card catalog, perusing the subject heading *vegetarianism*, I hardly anticipated the gem I soon would bring to light. The first printing of *Radical Vegetarianism* in 1981 also marked the first publication of these passages selected from the whole, either in German or in English. Special thanks is due the librarians of the Special Collection, without whose help the shroud surrounding this manuscript would never have been known. Permission to publish these segments was sought from all those even remotely involved in the donation of *Animals, My Brethren* to the University. But, alas, they had died, or had been forgotten by others, or had themselves forgotten. This essay, however, is not forgotten. Thirty years after its first publication here in this book, other books and numerous websites have reprinted either my selections or the entire essay. Edgar Kupfer shall remain forever freed.

M. M. B.

"Animals, My Brethren"

by Edgar Kupfer-Koberwitz

T HE FOLLOWING PAGES were written in the Concentration Camp Dachau, in the midst of all kinds of cruelties. They were furtively scrawled in a hospital barrack where I stayed during my illness, in a time when Death grasped day by day after us, when we lost twelve thousand within four and a half months.

Dear Friend:

You asked me why I do not eat meat and you are wondering at the reasons of my behavior. Perhaps you think I took a vow—some kind of penitence—denying me all the glorious pleasures of eating meat. You remember juicy steaks, succulent fishes, wonderfully tasted sauces, deliciously smoked ham and thousand wonders prepared out of meat, charming thousands of human palates; certainly you will remember the delicacy of roasted chicken. Now, you see, I am refusing all these pleasures and you think that only penitence, or a solemn vow, a great sacrifice could deny me that manner of enjoying life, induce me to endure a great resignment.

You look astonished, you ask the question: "But why and what for?" And you are wondering that you nearly guessed the very reason. But if I am, now, trying to explain you the very reason in one concise sentence, you will be astonished once more how far your guessing had been from my real motive. Listen to what I have to tell you:

I refuse to eat animals because I cannot nourish myself by the sufferings and by the death of other creatures. I refuse to do so, because I suffered so painfully myself that I can feel the pains of others by recalling my own sufferings.

I feel happy, nobody persecutes *me;* why should I persecute other beings or cause them to be persecuted?

I feel happy, I am no prisoner, I am free; why should I cause other creatures to be made prisoners and thrown into jail?

I feel happy, nobody harms me; why should I harm other creatures or have them harmed?

I feel happy, nobody wounds me; nobody kills me; why should I wound or kill other creatures or cause them to be wounded or killed for my pleasure and convenience?

Is it not only too natural that I do not inflict on other creatures the same thing which, I hope and fear, will never be inflicted on me? Would it not be most unfair to do such things for no other purpose than for enjoying a trifling physical pleasure at the expense of others' sufferings, others' deaths?

These creatures are smaller and more helpless than I am, but can you imagine a reasonable man of noble feelings who would like to base on such a difference a claim or right to abuse the weakness and the smallness of others? Don't you think that it is just the bigger, the stronger, the superior's duty to protect the weaker creatures instead of persecuting them, instead of killing them? "Noblesse oblige." I want to act in a noble way.

I recall the horrible epoch of inquisition and I am sorry to state that the time of tribunals for heretics has not yet passed by, that day by day, men use to cook in boiling water other creatures which are helplessly given in the hands of their torturers. I am horrified by the idea that such men are civilized people, no rough barbarians, no natives. But in spite of all, they are only primitively civilized, primitively adapted to their cultural environment. The average European, flowing over with highbrow ideas and beautiful speeches, commits all kinds of cruelties, smilingly, not because he is compelled to do so, but because he wants to do so. Not because he lacks the faculty to reflect upon and to realize all the dreadful things they are performing. Oh no! Only because they do not want to see the facts. Otherwise they would be troubled and worried in their pleasures.

It is quite natural what people are telling you. How could they do otherwise? I hear them telling about experiences, about utilities, and I know that they consider certain acts related to slaughtering as unavoidable. Perhaps they succeeded to win you over. I guess that from your letter.

Still, considering the necessities only, one might, perhaps, agree with such people. But is there really such a necessity? The thesis may be contested. Perhaps there exists still some kind of necessity for such persons who have not yet developed into full conscious personalities.

I am not preaching to them. I am writing this letter to you, to an already awakened individual who rationally controls his impulses, who feels responsible—internally and externally— of his acts, who knows that our supreme court is sitting in our conscience. There is no appellate jurisdiction against it.

Is there any necessity by which a fully self-conscious man can be induced to slaughter? In the affirmative, each individual may have the courage to do it by his own hands. It is, evidently, a miserable kind of cowardice to pay other people to perform the blood-stained job, from which the normal man refrains in horror and dismay. Such servants are given some farthings for their bloody work, and one buys from them the desired parts of the killed anima—if possible prepared in such a way that it does not any more recall the discomfortable circumstances, nor the animal, nor its being killed, nor the bloodshed.

I think that men will be killed and tortured as long as animals are killed and tortured. So long there will be wars, too. Because killing must be trained and perfected on smaller objects, morally and technically.

I see no reason to feel outraged by what others are doing, neither by the great nor by the smaller acts of violence and cruelty. But, I think, it is high time to feel outraged by all the small and great acts of violence and cruelty which we perform ourselves. And because it is much easier to win the smaller battles than the big ones, I think we should try to get over first our own trends towards smaller violence and cruelty, to avoid, or better, to overcome them once and for all. Then the day will come when it will be easy for us to fight and to overcome even the great cruelties. But we are still sleeping, all of us, in habitudes and inherited attitudes. They are like a fat, juicy sauce which helps us to swallow our own cruelties without tasting their bitterness.

I have not the intention to point out with my finger at this and that, at definite persons and definite situations. I think it is much more my duty to stir up my own conscience in smaller matters, to try to understand other people better, to get better and less selfish. Why should it be impossible then to act accordingly with regard to more important issues?

That is the point: I want to grow up into a better world where a higher law grants more happiness, in a new world where God's commandment reigns:

You Shall Love Each Other.

References

To a man whose mind is free there is something even more intolerable in the sufferings of animals than in the sufferings of man. For with the latter it is at least admitted that suffering is evil and that the man who causes it is a criminal. But thousands of animals are uselessly butchered every day without a shadow of remorse. If any man were to refer to it, he would be thought ridiculous. And that is the unpardonable crime. That alone is the justification of all that men may suffer.

> Romain Rolland
> *Jean-Christophe: Journey's End,*
> a section shortly before "The New Dawn"

THE VEGETARIAN AMONG CARNIVORES sometimes eats alone, and might be thought ridiculous for it. In the bodily sense the solitude is quite definite: not even a cow or fish or chicken shares the table. But in the spiritual sense the prose of philosophers and the praise of poets accompany the meal along with the blessings of the cow and fish and chicken and the silent perfect egg. Those statements of sentiment that have prefaced or unified these chapters are by no means exhaustive and were limited in number only by the chapters themselves. The works from which they were drawn are commonly called classics, so no extensive description of them is needed here. New editions are issued almost every decade, and the few no longer in print can be found in most university libraries and sometimes on the web.

In addition to the Bible (The Revised Standard Version),
these venerable authors and their worthy works were quoted:

Blake, "Auguries of Innocence"
Brecht, "Writing the Truth: Five Difficulties"
Butler, *Erewhon*
Ibsen, *Enemy of the People*
Kafka, "Investigations of a Dog"
Montaigne, "Apology for Raimond Sebond"
Nietzsche, *The Gay Science* and *The Genealogy of Morals*
Pasolini, "A Desperate Vitality"
Plato, *Crito* and *Theaetetus*
Plutarch, "The Eating of Meat"
Porphyry, *On Abstinence from Animal Food*
Rolland, *Jean-Christophe*
Schopenhauer, *On the Basis of Morality*; *Parerga and Paralipomena*, and *The World as Will and Representation*
Schweitzer, *Reverence for Life*
Singer, *Animal Liberation*
Mary Shelley, *Frankenstein*
Percy Shelley, "A Vindication of Natural Diet"
Steiner, "Problems of Nutrition"
Tolstoy, "The First Step"
Voltaire, *Candide*

Nearly half of these authors were not themselves vegetarians, but one need not be a vegetarian to recognize its merits
and to enlist with its ideology. Vegetarian or not, such a dos-
sier as the above may be more useful in constructing a case for
prosecution than in conducting a scholarly investigation of a
serious subject. For the latter we must turn from the philosophers and poets to the nutritionists.

As plant fiber sprinkled with soy-based ink, the pages of these books contain little nutritional value. We read nutrition books; we eat nutritious foods; we become wise and well fed; and then we become corpses. Then our survivors can add some spice to our lives, and feed our bodies to the turkey vultures of Death Valley, or to the timber wolves of the Yukon, or to the alligators of the Everglades. No point in wasting good food.

As we disappear through the teeth of time, these very pages can serve as paper napkins for lupine lips and crocodile smiles. See you later as an alligator.